contents

about the author

Vicki Courtney is an author and speaker with a ministry that reaches more than 150,000 people a year through events, books, and online resources. A mother of three, she seeks to provide women and parents with the tools necessary to navigate today's culture. She has done hundreds of radio and newspaper interviews, appearing on CNN, Fox News, and CNN Headline News as a youth culture commentator. In addition to being a national speaker, Vicki is a best-selling author of *5 Conversations You Must Have With Your Daughter*; *5 Conversations You Must Have With Your Son*; *Your Girl*; *Your Boy*; *TeenVirtue*; and *Between God and Me*. Interact with Vicki on her blog (*www.vicki courtney.com*) and follow her on Facebook, Twitter, and Instagram.

Of all her accomplishments, Vicki is most proud of being a wife and mother. A graduate of the University of Texas, Vicki is married to Keith and resides in Austin, Texas, where all three children live as well. Their oldest child, Ryan, and his wife, Casey, are Auburn graduates, as are daughter, Paige, and her husband, Matt. Hayden, the youngest, is a student at the University of Texas. Keith and Vicki recently became grandparents to Walker (Ryan and Casey's son).

Vicki enjoys running, shoe shopping, spending time at the lake with her family, and spoiling her grandson rotten. She is also quite fond of her two pint-sized Yorkshire terriers, Lexie and Scout, who she claims are the additional children her husband refused to have.

ever after

life lessons learned in my castle of chaos

vicki courtney

LifeWay Press®
Nashville, Tennessee

Published by LifeWay Press®
© Copyright 2013 Vicki Courtney

The author is represented by the literary agency of Alive Communications, Inc., 7680 Goddard St.,
Suite 200, Colorado Springs, CO 80920. *www.alivecommunications.com.*

ISBN 978-1-4158-7772-2
Item 005588688
Dewey decimal classification 248.843
Subject headings WOMEN \ GOD \ CHRISTIAN LIFE

Unless indicated otherwise, all Scripture quotations are taken from the Holman Christian Standard
Bible Copyright © 1999, 2000, 2002, 2003, 2009 by Holman Bible Publishers. Used by permission.
Holman Christian Standard Bible® and HCSB® are federally registered trademarks of Holman Bible
Publishers. Scripture marked ESV are taken from the Holy Bible, English Standard Version (ESV),
copyright © 2000, 2001 by Crossway Bibles, a division of Good News Publishers. Used by permission.
All rights reserved. Scripture quotations marked CEV are from the Contemporary English Version
Copyright © 1991, 1992, 1995 by American Bible Society. Used by permission. Scripture marked NIV
are taken from the Holy Bible, NEW INTERNATIONAL VERSION®. Copyright © 1973, 1978, 1984
by Biblica, Inc. All rights reserved worldwide. Used by permission. Scripture marked NASB are taken
from the New American Standard Bible®, Copyright © 1960, 1962, 1963, 1968, 1971, 1972, 1973, 1975,
1977, 1995 by the Lockman Foundation. Used by permission (*www.lockman.org*).

To order additional copies of this resource, write to LifeWay Church Resources, Customer Service, One
LifeWay Plaza, Nashville, TN 37234-0113; fax 615.251.5933; phone 800.458.2772; order online at *www.
lifeway.com* or email *orderentry@lifeway.com;* or visit the LifeWay Christian Store serving you.

Printed in the United States of America

Adult Ministry Publishing
LifeWay Church Resources
One LifeWay Plaza
Nashville, TN 37234-0152

about the study

In this return to the fun but unrealistic motif of fairy tales, women will begin to see how their expectations about life seldom match reality—and how God's desire and plan for our lives are so much better. While culture uplifts fairy-tale happy endings and the bigger-than-life people who live them, real life is quite different. It's tough out there and women need support from other women of faith. An *Ever After Bible Study* group can provide encouragement as you navigate the joys and pitfalls of godly living in a world that seemingly has lost its focus on God.

A recent empty nester, Vicki Courtney draws on valuable life lessons learned in the trenches of marriage and motherhood. True to her signature style, Vicki addresses challenges as a fellow Christian, wife, and mom who, on her best days, is a work in progress. She shares mistakes made, lessons learned, and memories forged along the way—plus the consistent promise from Scripture that God meets and empowers us wherever we are in the journey.

This study is developed around six group sessions with Vicki's video teaching, review, mutual support, and home study during the week. Just as Vicki taught and interacted with women around her dining room table, so can you use this study in one or more homes, an office setting, coffee shop, and classrooms at the church. Invite a friend or neighbor to join you and talk about insights together.

Five weeks of home study allow time to think about personal applications and to immerse yourself in Scripture. Abiding in Him and learning more about His plan for your life are priorities in *Ever After Bible Study*. Journaling can help you see how God is at work. Or you may want to make notes in this book and look back to see how your faith, family, or marriage is beginning to change for the better.

Ideally, a group meets for 75-90 minutes each week (or every other week), but if you have less time, eliminate some activities. A church leader or a mom or a group member can facilitate a group using the suggestions on pages 165-174. Customize them for the needs of your group.

Pray about your role and participation in this study. Make a commitment to see what God has in store for you. Pray for the other participants and for where God will take all of you during this six-week journey together.

meet Vicki's group

Vicki and Keith Courtney teach a group of young marrieds on Sundays at their Austin church. They love being involved in these couples' lives, building deep relationships through a common bond in Christ. So Vicki invited eight women, all from the Austin area, to join her around the dining room table. Each brings a unique perspective to the *Ever After Bible Study* message—just as your group will bring "to the table" their unique needs, insights about Scripture, and joys and sorrows. Meet this group now and enjoy their contributions throughout the study.

Tami Overhauser is originally from California, where she met and married her husband, Chad. They've been married for 15 years. Tami is a stay-at-home mother of four—Rebekah, age 14; Samantha, 12; Adam, 8; and David. 6.

Carrie Betzen, married to Brian for 10 years, has been blessed with two beautiful daughters—Addison, age 4, and McKenna, 2½. She does part-time marketing communications work. For fun, Carrie enjoys running, exercising, reading, baking, and vacationing in tropical places.

Kati Smith has been married to her wonderful husband, Ken, for almost 18 years. God blessed them with two precious sons—Kolton, age 7, and Kooper, 4—after their lengthy struggle with infertility. Kati loves spending time with family and friends, as well as cooking, entertaining, and traveling.

Lyndsey Testone is a stay-at-home mother of three—Kate, age 8; Jack, 5; and Meg, 9 months. Lyndsey and Stephen have been married for 10 great years. She and Jaclyn Benson, also in the group, are sisters.

Jaclyn Benson, originally from Austin, graduated from the University of Mary Hardin–Baylor, where she met her husband, Mark. Married for seven years, Jaclyn and Mark have a seven-month-old daughter named Emma.

Shelly Gleason describes herself as an Austin native. She attended the University of Texas at Austin, where she met her husband, Robert. Married for 15 years, they have been blessed with a beautiful daughter named Abby. Shelly enjoys being a wife and mother and she loves Jesus with all her heart.

Anna Jenkins calls herself a daughter, sister, wife, mother, auntie, Christian, and friend. She loves online shopping, barbeque, coordinating shoes in every color, big jewelry, baking (not cooking), entertaining, sweet tea, professional football, Swedish Fish candy, and decorating Americana-style. Anna and Marcus have been married since 1999 and welcomed Abigayle in 2008.

Absent when this photo was taken is Natalie Bibler, who was part of the small group during DVD sessions 1, 5, and 6. Natalie is married to Josh and they have two boys—Jaden, age 6, and Brody, 4. Married for nine years, she serves as a preschool director for Canyon Creek Preschool.

Standing, left to right: Casey Courtney (on-site coordinator), Tami, Kati, Lyndsey, Shelly, Chris Watson (assistant)
Seated, left to right: Carrie, Vicki and Scout, Jaclyn, and Anna

As is always the case, an awesome crew was doing their work behind the cameras, off-site, or in post-production. For those who don't look at video credits, thanks here to Rick Simms, Lisa Turner, Adrian Alverson, Jimmy Patterson, Greg Smith, Paul Lopez, Steve Fralick, and Mike Psanos.

Week 1

fairy-tale letdown

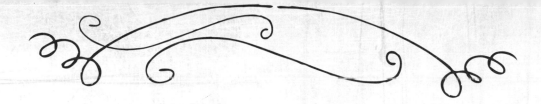

"If you happen to read fairy tales, you will observe that one idea runs from one end of them to the other—the idea that peace and happiness can only exist on some condition. This idea, which is the core of ethics, is the core of the nursery-tales."

G.K. Chesterton

The Spirit himself bears witness with our spirit that we are children of God, and if children, then heirs—heirs of God and fellow heirs with Christ.
Romans 8:16-17, ESV

DVD session 1

Today's group: Anna Jenkins, Carrie Betzen, Natalie Bibler, Tami Overhauser

QUESTION: Think of a time when the memory and the fairy tale did not match.

A fairy-tale pursuit is really a _____ _____ .

1 John 2:15-17

A fairy tale puts us at the center of the story.

Love of the world _____ _____ _____ for the Father (The Message).

Three predominant _____ of our nature:

- Desire of the _____

- Desire of the _____

- Pride in _____

Desire of the flesh = **epithumia** (*ep-ee-thoo-mee´-ah*): a *longing*, esp. for what is forbidden—lust (after)

Desire of the eyes = **ophthalmos** (*of-thal-mos´*): *vision; envy*; (from the jealous side glance) basis of our word *ophthalmology*

Ecclesiastes 6:9

QUESTION: What is your biggest area of struggle?

God has wired us for a bigger, better story than any fairy tale—a story that _____ _____ .

Every girl wants the fairy tale. And by fairy tale, I mean the works: the prince, the castle, and, eventually, the little royal subjects running down the castle corridors in matching smocked rompers.

And let's not forget the personal attendants who come as part of Cinderella's dream package.

Discuss together

Throughout this study you will meet eight women who are part of the Bible study group Vicki and her husband, Keith, teach at their church. She asks her small group for their responses to certain questions. You may want to stop the video and answer these questions too.

Other questions to consider include:

In what ways have you gotten comfortable with life as it is now?

As a believer, how do you juggle living in the world yet not pursuing things of the world?

Downloads of this session are available at *www.lifeway.com*.

Day 1

Once upon a Time

Romans 8:18-25

As mentioned in the video, every girl wants the fairy tale. The details may vary from princess to princess, but the end goal is the same: happily ever after.

If you need proof of the fairy-tale pursuit, look no further than Pinterest. Women of all ages and stages of life are pinning their fairy-tale hopes and dreams on virtual pinboards. Long before Prince Charming arrives on the scene, many women have pinned their dream weddings down to the fine details. And heaven help poor Prince Charming when he does show up and eventually takes a peek at Cinderella's engagement ring pinboard. He may hop on his white horse and gallop outta town, clutching his wallet with white knuckles.

Once we are married, the fairy-tale dream continues. My daughter is newly married and has an entire pinboard devoted to "Future Little McMichens." I couldn't help but smile when I saw it.

Pinterest wasn't around when I began writing the dream script for my fairy tale. I remember spending the night with my best girlfriend in grade school and devoting endless amounts of time to naming our future children. For the record, I was going to have twin girls named Tiffany and Stephanie. I'm fairly certain we embraced the concept of the stork delivering them to our doorsteps, given that boys still had cooties. I never did get those twin girls, but as many of us have learned by now, real life doesn't always measure up to our fairy-tale expectations.

Recall

When you were a little girl, how did you imagine your life as an adult? Do you recall dreaming about marriage and motherhood?

What factors influenced your fairy-tale dream over the years?

Describe the moment when you realized real life wasn't going to measure up to your fairy-tale expectations.

Read

The truth is, we don't live in Disneyland. Not even close. One glance at the nightly news, one step on the scale, one new scandal on Wall Street—all remind us of that truth. In theological terms, we live in a fallen world. In personal terms, life is hard.

Read Romans 8:18-25.
What does this passage tell you about life on earth right now?

Based on what you read in these verses, describe the created world. Use as many adjectives as possible.

In verse 18, Paul talked about the glory that will be revealed in us. What do you think that will look like?

In verse 20, Paul indicates that the creation was subjected to something. To what was he referring? _____. Read this verse in several Bible translations to see other words that are used.

In verse 23, Paul indicated that believers are eagerly waiting for adoption. Put yourself in the shoes of a child (or parent) who desperately awaits an adoption to be finalized.

Compare that feeling with the waiting Paul described in verse 23.

How does this understanding impact the meaning of the verse for you?

Reread verses 24-25 and express them in your own words.

What role does hope play in your nonfairy-tale life? What role should it play in your life?

The Book of Romans is unlike any other letter Paul wrote. While other epistles were written to address problems in the many young churches popping up in the first century after Christ's resurrection, this book was written to give the Roman church a solid foundation of the crucial basics of the Christian faith. In penning it, Paul provided the church (and us) the total message of Christianity. Almost every Christian doctrine can be found in this book, including living as redeemed people in a fallen world.

Paul used some powerful words to describe our presence in this world—words like "sufferings," "futility," "bondage," "corruption," "groaning," and "labor pains" (let's not forget he was a single guy!). These verses are a stark reminder that our lives here as we await Christ's return are not a trip to the Magic Kingdom.

Let's look at one word in particular: futility. Other translations use words like "vanity" (KJV), "curse"(New Living), "frustration"(NIV), "frailty"(Amplified), and "confusion" (CEV). These do not paint a fairy-tale, perfect portrait of our lives. In fact, they demonstrate just how much our lives are *not* like we thought they would be when we were little girls with dreams of Prince Charming, the castle, and royal subjects running underfoot.

The things of this world—"the lust of the flesh, the lust of the eyes, and the pride in one's lifestyle"—are not intended to satisfy (1 John 2:16). Our fairy-tale dreams cannot be fulfilled this side of heaven because, well, we're not in heaven yet. We were designed by our Creator for more than this life provides, and when we rely on the stuff of this world to completely satisfy us, we'll be disappointed.

When we expect others to complete us, we'll wind up disillusioned, discouraged, and, many times, divorced. When the next outfit or the next gadget becomes the next "fix" to soothe the deep aching in our hearts, we find ourselves in debt and still in despair. Why? Because God created within the human heart the need for communion with Himself, and until that can take place in a perfect place, we will "groan within ourselves" (Rom. 8:23).

Until then, what do we do? How do we respond to the sobering recognition that this life, however grand or glorious or exciting or picture-perfect, will ultimately disappoint us?

- We can deny that there is anything beyond this life. That's certainly what many people opt to do—deny the afterlife; ignore the existence of God; convince themselves that the ache isn't really there, that they really are happy. That may work for a while, but the yearning for more than this world has to offer will return.

- We can self-medicate to soothe the ache. We can medicate with drugs and alcohol, with as much stuff as we can accumulate and pile in self-storage buildings, with unhealthy relationships that demand more than they can ever provide, with children who provide a second chance to correct our own youthful mistakes.

- The worst response we can have to this ever-present ache is to get comfortable with it. Like the proverbial frog in the pot of increasingly hot water, we sit in our surroundings, never realizing that being comfortable in our environment is actually killing us. Let's not forget, the frog has the ability to jump out at any given time. So why doesn't he? The change is so subtle and gradual that the frog fails to see the danger of his familiar environment.

Are we any different? We settle, we stop seeking the Divine, we convince ourselves that this is the best it'll ever be, so we stay put in our current circumstances. And just like that, we stop living.

The alternative is to live in hope. Like a woman separated from her beloved, we ache and we hope and we read His Love Letter (Scripture) over and over, looking for nuances we missed before. And, above all, we remain faithful.

We remember that eventually we will be reunited with our Lover and that our "sufferings of this present time are not worth comparing with the glory" (Rom. 8:18) that we will experience.

Until then, we hope and we wait.

"If we find ourselves with a desire that nothing in this world can satisfy, the most probable explanation is that we were made for another world." —C.S. Lewis, *Mere Christianity*

What about you? How have you tried to satisfy the longing in your heart? In what ways have you gotten comfortable with life as is?

Respond

How did God speak to you today?

What is your response to Him?

Day 2

Prince-Not-So-Charming

Revelation 4:1-11

Someday our prince will come. We grew up tucking that promise away in our hearts as part of the dream. For the record, my prince arrived in August 1985 at a Christian weekend retreat for college students. Much like the fairy tales, it was love at first sight.

Well, for me, at least. He clearly hadn't read the script in which the love-at-first-sight thing was mutual.

I recall a particularly low moment when Keith called me in the weeks after our first meeting and asked me for a friend's phone number. Where was that scene in my fairy-tale script?! (I soothed my heartache by sobbing into my pillow and listening to Air Supply for two hours. And I may or may not have given him the wrong number.)

He finally came to his senses, and we recently celebrated our twenty-fifth wedding anniversary. It's safe to say I carried my perfect-prince expectations into my first few years of marriage, even though it didn't take long for the prince to fall off the pedestal I had put him on. Or, rather, the one I pushed him from. He was a bit slow adjusting to the part of the charming prince.

I doubt Mr. Darcy (*Pride and Prejudice*) would have left Mrs. Darcy to play in a church league softball tournament on the day they brought their first child home from the hospital. Or that Mr. Darcy would have called his mother to ask how to get the mildew smell out of the towels.

And I'm still waiting for him to cup my face in his hands and tell me, "You have bewitched me body and soul and I love ... I love ... I love you." I don't think I've ever even heard him use the word "bewitched" in the twenty-five years we've been married. "Witch" maybe, but I digress.

Recall

What expectations did you have about marriage and Prince Charming?

If you are married, describe a time when you realized your Prince Charming could sometimes be a toad.

Think about a time when someone deeply disappointed you. How did you respond?

Read

On day 1 you read and reflected on the truth that we live in a fallen world. One consequence of the fall is difficulty in relationships, especially with our spouses. Remember what happened when Adam and Eve ate the forbidden fruit?

Read Genesis 3:16-19.
What consequence did Eve face because of her sin?

What did those consequences focus on?

What consequences did Adam face because of his sin?

What did his consequences focus on?

Adam's consequences centered around work. Think about that for a moment. Where does a typical guy find fulfillment and a sense of purpose and worth? His job. That is often the biggest source of a guy's joy—and of his disappointment and frustration.

Around what did Eve's consequences center? Two primary relationships—with her husband and with her children. Think about that. Where does a typical woman find the greatest sense of fulfillment and joy? In her relationships, specifically with her husband. And where does a woman often find her biggest source of anguish, frustration, and disappointment? Yep, in her relationship with her husband.

So what causes this deep sense of longing and disappointment in so many women? Why do so many women seem so unfulfilled, cynical, bitter, and downright despondent over their relationship with their husband? Because we mistakenly think our husband should fulfill our heart's desire and make our lives complete.

Do you remember the movie *Jerry McGuire*? Of course you do. Romance. Laughter. That handsome lead man (back before he took a ride on the crazy train and jumped up and down on a sofa on live TV). Everything a woman wants in a chick flick. One of the most critical—and misguided— scenes in the movie takes place in an elevator. Jerry and Dorothy are watching a deaf couple communicating with each other when they see the man sign something to the woman, something that earns him a passionate kiss.

While Jerry has no idea what has been said, Dorothy fills him in (because her aunt is hearing impaired). He signed, "You complete me."

Of course, in true fairy-tale form, Jerry sweeps into a room full of women at the end of the movie and proclaims his undying love to Dorothy, using that three-word sentence. And they live happily ever after.

The truth of the matter is, no man can ever complete you. A man can complement you; he can be strong in areas in which you struggle. He can be a great cook or a great checkbook keeper or a patient father. God often puts us together (some-times humorously, I think) so that our weaknesses and strengths play off (and annoy) each other.

But no man can ever make you complete. Why? Because you were not primarily created for a relationship with a man.

Read Colossians 1:16-17.
According to these verses, who created you and why?

Did you catch that? "All things have been created *through Him and for Him*" (v. 16, italics added). You were created for Him, for a relationship with Him. Yes, you were created for relationships with other people; God told Adam he needed companionship. But in eternity, your relationship with your spouse will no longer be as significant.

Stop for a minute and think about the irony of that truth. We spend so much time on this earth pining for a soul mate, trying to manufacture someone into a soul mate, and expressing disappointment about a soul mate (or lack thereof). Could it be that our affections are misguided?

Read Revelation 4:1-11.

What is pictured in this scene? List some of the descriptions.

Who is seated on the throne?

What happens around the throne?

Summarize verse 11. Compare it to Colossians 1:16-17.

How does this passage give you perspective on your human relationships?

If I didn't know John was writing Revelation under the direction of the Holy Spirit, I'd certainly wonder about him. An emerald rainbow. Twenty-four thrones and twenty-four elders. Flashes of lightning. Fiery torches. A sea of glass. Creatures with eyes in the front and the back and six wings.

Why such odd descriptions? Because sometimes, words are just inadequate. I think John was overwhelmed by what he saw. He was struck dumb by the vision before him and what he ended up writing down was just the tip of the iceberg. Those were the only words he could come up with. The scene is dramatic. The stuff of science fiction. J.R.R. Tolkien couldn't have envisioned anything greater.

At the center of it all is "the One seated on the throne, the One who lives forever and ever" (v. 9). Only in verse 11 is "the One" identified: "Our Lord and God." Why use that description? Why not just call Him any of the other names in the Old or New Testaments? Adonai. Yahweh. Jehovah. Emmanuel. El Shaddai. Elohim. King of kings. Lord of lords. Any of these would be readily understood by the first-century readers who ended up with John's writing.

So what's the big deal with "the One"?

Perhaps because no matter the situation, He is "the One." Not "the one" the fairy tales program us to dream about. He is the only One—the only One who will never disappoint, betray, or belittle. He is the only One who completely understands us from the inside out (Ps. 139). He is the only One who can meet our every need, heal our every hurt, and dismantle every barrier we've put up around ourselves. He is the only One, "though the earth trembles and the mountains topple into the depths of the seas" (Ps. 46:2), who will remain. Faithful. Forgiving. Flawless. Patient. Providing. Perfector. Healing. Helping. Hoping. Holy. Holding. Gracious. Giving. Glorious. Redeeming. Restoring. Saving. Supporting. Sovereign. Satisfying. He is the One our hearts seek.

There's no Prince Charming, no man on that throne. Because He alone is the True Prince. And He alone can fulfill our heart's desire.

Reflect

What unrealistic expectations have you placed on your husband (or others) to meet your needs?

What desires of your heart need the fulfilling that only the Only One can provide?

Respond

How did God speak to you today?

What is your response to Him?

Day 3

Misplaced Passions and Pursuits

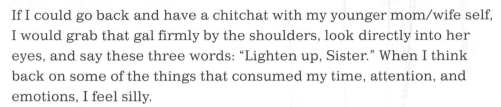

Psalm 27:4; Matthew 22:34-40

If I could go back and have a chitchat with my younger mom/wife self, I would grab that gal firmly by the shoulders, look directly into her eyes, and say these three words: "Lighten up, Sister." When I think back on some of the things that consumed my time, attention, and emotions, I feel silly.

During the year I'm thinking of, I spent more time trying to find perfectly coordinated Easter outfits for my children than reflecting on my risen Savior—so very silly. Or the time I went into a tailspin when my child was assigned to the new teacher … again … for the third year in a row—so very silly. Or the time I was in charge of planning the church women's retreat and obsessed over the details of the program—so very silly.

The list goes on and on of things I once considered to be urgent. Things that now seem … so very silly. If I could do it over again, I would lighten up and focus my time and energy on that one thing that mattered in the scheme of eternity. That one thing.

Recall

Describe a time when less-important priorities sent you running in every direction.

What are your priorities? List them.

How can you tell when your priorities are getting out of whack?

Read

On day 2, we discovered that God is the Only One who can meet our every need. Even though all things, including us, were created "through Him and for Him," we spend most of our time chasing after other things—even good things—that draw us away from our Priority. He ends up at the bottom of our list instead of at the top, directing everything else that should (or shouldn't) be on our list.

Read Psalm 27:4.

What words stand out to you in this verse? Why are they significant?

What was the psalmist's one desire?

What would he do in this place?

Why do you think the psalmist was so focused on this one thing?

This one little verse is packed with rich description when you break it down. The word "asked" means "to inquire, borrow, beg."[1] This is not a cursory request with little emotion behind it. Rather, picture your daughter begging you to let her go out with her friends. Or picture your son imploring you to buy that pair of tennis shoes because "the whole team" has them. This is desperation, gals.

So here's a question: what was the last thing you begged God for? The psalmist begged for one thing: "to dwell in the house of the Lord."

Really? That's what the psalmist wanted? To live at church? Likely, if you polled the average woman at church, you'd probably get something like, "Um, no. I'd rather have a break from church." For us, church can become a place of activity rather than refuge. Volunteer in preschool once a month. Teach a discipleship class. Attend a ladies' Bible study. Serve on a committee. Bake another casserole. Sunday morning has become a triathlon.

Remember, though, the psalmist didn't serve on any search committees. In the Old Testament, the temple was synonymous with the presence of God. Before the Spirit of God dwelled in you and me, He dwelt in the holy of holies. So what the psalmist was asking for was to be continually in God's presence. He wanted to gaze on the "beauty of the Lord," not stand around in a Sunday School class trying to look comfortable in dress shoes.

The word "gaze" can be translated as "to look upon; to contemplate, especially with pleasure, to delight in something."[2] Now *that's* something I can get excited about. And what did the psalmist want to gaze at, look at, delight in? The beauty of God. The word "beauty" in this verse carries much more meaning than we would typically use in everyday conversation. In a day of airbrushed models and the objectification of women, towering skyscrapers and concrete jungles, many of us have lost the understanding of true beauty. We have forgotten what it's like to see something that takes our breath away. But that's the picture here. The word means "kindness, pleasantness, delightfulness."[3] The psalmist's one request was to be in the presence of God, delighting in the character and nature of God. When was the last time you did that?

When was the last time God's presence took your breath away? When was the last time you delighted in the totality of God's indescribable character? When was the last time you were encouraged to seek Him that way? When was the last time your pastor preached on seeking God's beauty as the priority of your life?

Why do you think the psalmist asked for that one thing above all else? Solomon asked for wisdom. Elisha wanted a double portion of Elijah's blessing. Jacob wanted Esau's birthright. James and John wanted to sit on either side of Jesus in the kingdom. All great things, but they all fall short. But not David. He asked for intimate knowledge of God. Why?

Because that one thing—a right outlook on God and your relationship to Him—puts everything else in perspective. From that understanding, every other priority falls into place. Without continually being in the presence of God Almighty, nothing makes sense. Not your job. Not your relationships. Not your ministry to others. Not suffering. Not joy. Not the nightly news.

But when you spend time contemplating the Beginning and the End, the Alpha and Omega, the Author and Perfector of our faith, life finds its meaning and purpose. Vocation is a means to worship God. Relationships give us a taste of God's love. Ministry is not hard, but is simply pointing others to the One who has made your life complete.

Let's look at it another way. Read Matthew 22:34-40.

What question did the expert in the law ask Jesus?

What was Jesus' response? Break it down just as Jesus did.

Where did Jesus get this commandment? (You may have to look it up in a reference source.)

Why do you think God was so specific in using "with all" so many times?

What did Jesus add as the second commandment? What did He say about these two commandments?

Some background into Old Testament law might shed a little light on this encounter between the Legalist and the Minister of Grace (I wish we had the latter job on church staffs!). Originally, God gave His people the Ten Commandments. But in addition to those, He set into place ceremonial laws, regulations for sacrifices, tithes and offerings, diet, purification, religious festivals, and the Sabbath.

In addition to those written Scriptures, the Jews followed the Talmud—the interpretation of those laws—that was passed down from generation to generation until the laws were compiled and written down in the Mishnah. The result? By the time Jesus hit the scene, any good Jew would follow all of those laws—all 613 of them.[4] How in the world was Jesus supposed to choose the most important?

In true Jesus fashion, He skipped the trimmings and cut straight to the meat: love God with all your heart, all your soul, and all your mind. Then love others. Don't get those confused.

At the risk of taking Scripture out of context, let me put everything together. What is that one thing you should be seeking? What is the most important commandment? What is your priority, that one thing that takes precedence over everything?

Loving God with all of your heart, soul, mind, and strength. Gazing on the beauty of the Lord and seeking Him.

Does it seem a bit simplistic? Maybe it is. Or maybe it is just singular. The one thing that should characterize our lives above all is our relationship with Jesus. Unfortunately, most of us have muddied that with a thousand other priorities—volunteering, shopping, gossip, technology, fashion, footwear, discipling our kids, loving our husband, going to church.

At the risk of sounding heretical, let me say this: your primary responsibility is not raising your kids. It's not even loving and serving your husband. Your first priority is your relationship with God.

He is your priority.

Period.

Reflect

What other priorities—good or bad—have gotten in the way of your ultimate priority?

Why does making Him your priority often seem so difficult to pursue?

Respond

How did God speak to you today?

What is your response to Him?

Day 4
Lost and Found
Matthew 6:19-24

Back before I was a speaker and author, I had a rather unusual job. I sold loose diamonds to prospective grooms who were in the market for an engagement ring. I had stumbled into the business while in college, working part-time for a diamond broker. What began as a great part-time gig translated into a thriving stay-at-home mommy job. My kids grew up thinking it was normal for moms to sell diamonds across the kitchen table while they watched a steady stream of cartoons in the family room.

One of my first customers bought a beautiful 1.5-carat round diamond and chose a simple tiffany solitaire mounting. He was in a hurry to propose that weekend, so I told him I would rush the diamond over to my craftsman to be mounted as soon as my son woke up from his morning nap. I tucked the diamond (wrapped in its original white papers) in a simple lunch sack and placed it into my son's diaper bag.

Once I arrived at the craftsman's office, I put my son into the stroller and the diaper bag into the basket at the stroller's base. I wheeled him past a crowd of people waiting outside a popular lunch spot.

Once inside the craftsman's studio, I reached down for the lunch sack in the diaper bag and, to my horror, discovered it wasn't there! I will never forget my panic in that moment. I dumped the entire contents of the diaper bag on the floor. No lunch sack. I asked the craftsman to watch my baby as I raced out the door to retrace my steps.

When I arrived at the car, there sat the lunch sack next to the curb in front of the restaurant. Many lunch patrons had probably stepped right over the paper sack, unaware that it contained a treasure worth far more than the lunch they were waiting for. I grabbed the sack and said a silent prayer before peeking inside. The diamond was uninsured, so I would have had to replace the stone myself—$6,000 we didn't have. I opened the sack and, praise God, found my diamond and some massive relief.

I will never forget that day. My customer could propose. My baby could go to college. My husband would never have to know. The lost treasure was found. I could breathe again.

Recall

When's the last time you went on a treasure hunt for something? What was the object? Why were you seeking it so desperately?

How did you feel when the object was finally found?

Read

Scripture records its own treasure hunt of sorts. Rather than a search for a bargain on designer shoes or a discount price on flooring, the pursuit described by Jesus is of a much more urgent nature. Check it out for yourself.

Read Matthew 6:19-24.

Now don't turn away because you're already familiar with this passage. Stop and ask God to give you a fresh perspective on this chunk of truth.

Skim verses 1-18.

What has Jesus been talking about prior to this part of His sermon? (Remember, this is part of the Sermon on the Mount, so consider it as one block of Scripture—not to be divorced from its parts.)

What did Jesus caution His listeners to guard against
in the first few verses?

Why would Jesus connect "treasures in heaven" (Matt. 6:20) with giving
to the needy, prayer, and fasting? Seems a bit disconnected, doesn't it?

What did Jesus teach listeners to guard against collecting? In what did
Jesus advise them to collect instead? What does that look like?

How do verses 22-23 relate to verses 19-21 and 24?

If you have been involved in a church for any length of time, you've probably
heard a Bible study or sermon on this passage of Scripture. In fact, you may be
so familiar with it that you've gotten a little complacent, with an "I already know
what this is talking about" attitude. But let's dig a little deeper. You might be
surprised. And convicted.

As a backdrop to these verses, it's important to note that Jesus' teaching on treasures, wealth, and earthly possessions was controversial. Only the most radical
sages in His day taught that possessions were essentially worthless. Traditional
Jewish teachers taught that material wealth was a sign of God's favor. Most "holy"
people loved to gather up their stuff and put it on display for all to see how God
had highly blessed them. In this sermon, Jesus turns this thinking on its head.

Verse 19 contains an interesting word: "store" (NASB). Your Bible might say "collect" or "lay up" or "place" or even "treasure." At first glance, that's what the word
means. But it carries a metaphorical meaning too. It means "so to live from day to
day as to increase either the bitterness or the happiness of one's consequent lot."[5]

In other words, that which is stored determines your emotional state—good or
bad. Jesus was cautioning against storing up stuff that could get taken away, and

thus change your emotional outcome. It's pretty savvy advice, especially for those of us who live in such opulence. And compared to the rest of the world, we all live in opulence.

What's interesting is this: the same word "store" is used in verse 20, where Jesus told us to store up treasures in heaven. The theologian Matthew Henry put it this way: "Christ counsels to make our best things the joys and glories of the other world, those things not seen which are eternal, and to place our happiness in them."[6] Ask yourself, *What would it be like to live with such singleness of focus that my heavenly treasure determines the increase of my bitterness or my happiness?*

So what exactly is a treasure? Certainly in this materialistic American culture, our first inclination is to think of stuff—but "treasures" can be defined much more broadly than that. Even the poorest person can be guilty of hoarding and seeking the wrong treasures. For instance, do you seek after the honor that comes with having a "perfect" child? Does your daughter have to make the cheerleading team or be an A student? Does she need to wear designer clothes and fit in with the cool crowd?

Perhaps the treasure you seek is a slim figure. How much time do you spend working out, looking for low-fat recipes, and comparing yourself to other women?

This simple question will reveal what your treasure is: what dictates your mood?

What causes you to swing radically from peacefulness to outright despair? That's your treasure. Speaking of treasure, Jesus had something to say about it and why seeking the right one is so critical:

"For where your treasure is, there your heart will be also" (Matt. 6:21).

No wonder people either loved Jesus or hated Him. He didn't leave any wiggle room. The treasures you accumulate—those things you seek after every day— carry your heart away with them.

This verse prompts a question:

What are your treasures? Or asked another way, where is your heart?

The answer is the same. Your treasure can be almost anything: a job, success, family, home, ministry, notoriety, ambition, obedient children, or a respectable husband. It can be the pride of being a working mom or a stay-at-home mom. It can be the status of homeschooling your children. It can be the applause you get from church members for volunteering for everything. It can be scrapbooking or making jewelry or reading. It can be an illicit affair or pornography. It can even be perfection or legalism. Your treasure is simply that thing that has captured your heart.

We've been reading about the greatest commandment to "love the Lord your God with all your heart, and with all your soul, and with all your mind" (Matt. 22:37). Why? Because God is the treasure.

That's why Jesus talked about the eye being so important. Of course, He wasn't talking about the ocular device we use to watch TV (although what we watch can make us full of darkness). The word Jesus uses for "good" in verse 22 is actually "single" in the original Greek. Think of it this way: if your focus is single—set on the things of God—then your heart is set on God alone. The problem is, most of us don't have a single focus. We are easily distracted by many other things, many treasures that look like pearls but are really just glitzy plastic. As a consequence, our hearts aren't fully His.

Reflect

"It would seem that Our Lord finds our desires not too strong, but too weak. We are half-hearted creatures, fooling about with drink and sex and ambition when infinite joy is offered us, like an ignorant child who wants to go on making mud pies in a slum because he cannot imagine what is meant by the offer of a holiday at the sea. We are far too easily pleased." —C.S. Lewis, *The Weight of Glory*

How does this quote parallel your study today?

With what have you become far too easily pleased? In other words, what has taken away your single focus on God?

Respond

How did God speak to you today?

What is your response to Him?

Day 5
First Loves
Revelation 2:1-7

I still have the note my "first love" passed me on the second day of fifth grade. We had known each other for two short days, but we shared a common bond. At recess, our class, along with three other fifth-grade classes, was told to run around the baseball backstops. Each day, the boy and girl to finish first would get to sit out the next day's runaround. I finished first one day along with a cute, shy, lanky boy with a moppy haircut who was also in my class.

Dorwin Malone was his name. While our classmates ran around the backstops on the next day, we sat nervously on the blacktop, stealing an occasional glance when we thought the other wasn't looking. Once we got back to class, he passed a note down the row of desks until it landed on my desktop. I opened it up and read:

I like you. Will you go with me? Circle yes or no.

I smiled and quickly drew a circle around yes, folded the note back up, and passed it back down the row. My head was spinning, my palms sweating, and I was fairly certain the teacher would hear my heart beating out of my chest and intercept my first shot at love. But the note arrived safely, and I got a shy smile in return. It was official. I was going steady.

For the better part of the year, Dorwin and I continued to reign as fastest boy and girl runners in the fifth grade. Our relationship was forged on the days we sat on the blacktop while our classmates did laps. And by forged, I mean we hardly exchanged a single word—just shy, awkward glances. What we couldn't say face-to-face, we scribbled bravely on notes that we continued to pass during class.

I have an entire shoebox full of those notes. In one, Dorwin asked if we could hold hands under the lunch table the following day. I circled yes again. I'm fairly certain I didn't sleep a wink that night. I can still remember the jolt of adrenalin when he would grab my hand under the table each and every day. I learned to eat my lunch with one hand and even scolded my mother for putting my sandwiches in fold-over lunch bags that required me to rip them open with my teeth.

My relationship with Dorwin lasted the entire school year and partly into the summer until Bobby the New Boy sat next to me at the Summer Movie Circus. He told one of my friends he liked me, and just like that, Dorwin was yesterday's news. Even so, his notes remain in my treasure box of memories. You never forget your first love.

Recall

Who was your first love as a child or a teenager? Describe some of the feelings experienced with your first taste of love.

How did the relationship end? What did you feel in the aftermath?

Read

We have been talking about our relationship with God. We discovered Him as our True Prince who should be our priority above all else. We also talked about how we are often so distracted by other things that we lose focus on Him and our heart goes elsewhere. Put another way, we've lost that loving feeling.

Read Revelation 2:1-7.
To whom is this letter written? How is Jesus described?

What positive things did Jesus note about the church at Ephesus?
What one criticism did Jesus offer about the church?

What things did Jesus tell the church to do in response?

What is the price of remaining loveless, according to verse 5? What does this tell you about the importance of love?

Jesus commended the church at Ephesus for several things. They had worked hard. They had endured hardship and trouble. They had rejected evil. They had been persecuted for their relationship with Christ and still remained faithful to Him. They had not grown weary.

By all outward appearances, that church was the model for all the others to follow. If that church had existed today, the senior pastor would have written a book. Other churches would have copied their model. They would have started satellite churches all over town, sponsored a church in Haiti, created a website, sold merchandise, and opened a coffee shop in the lobby. Except for one problem. And according to Jesus, it was a big problem: "I have this against you: you have abandoned the love you had at first."

Jesus' words echo what God said to the people of Israel through the prophet Jeremiah: "I remember the loyalty of your youth, your love as a bride—how you followed Me in the wilderness, in a land not sown" (Jer. 2:2).

The letter to the church at Ephesus is a constant reminder that you can do all the right things in the name of love without actually loving. It is possible to go to Bible studies, take casseroles to new moms, lead your children in the plan of salvation, and boycott every store that sells pornography without ever nurturing a growing love relationship with Jesus Christ.

It is possible to do a thousand things in the name of Christ without ever uttering a word of love toward Him. And according to Jesus, that's a problem.

Read Mark 7:5-7.
What was Jesus' criticism of the Pharisees?

The Pharisees had done everything right. They tithed. They worshiped at the temple. They helped the poor. They memorized the Torah. They observed all the rituals and kept themselves ceremonially clean. And Jesus' (paraphrased) response? "You hypocrites. You honor Me with your lips and your actions, but your hearts are far from Me." Remember the importance of the heart from your study yesterday? This is a really big deal.

Read 1 Corinthians 13:1-3. Complete these sentences (adapted from the Contemporary English Version).
If I could speak all languages of humans and of angels but didn't have love, _____ .
What if I could prophesy and understand all secrets and all knowledge? And if I had faith that moved mountains, but didn't have love, _____ .
If I gave away all that I owned and let myself be burned alive, but I didn't have love, _____ .

Yes, love is more than an emotion, but it's not just a bunch of actions. According to Scripture, you love first, then you act out of that love. The church at Ephesus had forgotten that along the way. They had completely abandoned love altogether. Is that possible? Apparently so. And it happens all the time in today's churches too. Have you ever been in a worship service in which the theology was right but you could sense no love for God or for others? Have you ever known a person who could quote Scripture verbatim but who seemed ice cold?

Let's get a little more personal. Have you ever been so busy doing things for God that you didn't have time to spend with God? God doesn't want your acts of service. He wants your heart. The rest will flow from that. So what is the solution?

Reread Revelation 2:5.
What three things did Jesus tell the church to do?

REMEMBER. Take a good, long look at your history with Jesus. What was it like when you felt the closest to Him? When did you start to abandon your love? What sequence of events in your life replaced your love for Him? Just as a trip down memory lane with your spouse helps rekindle the love you share, so can taking that same trip with Jesus help you remember your journey with Him.

Recall the times He has rescued you. Think about the answered prayers. Mull over the ways He has carried you, restored you, been patient with you, laughed with you, reminded you, protected you, provided for you, and sheltered you. These reflections can rekindle your love and make it even stronger.

REPENT. Stop doing what you were doing. Change your direction. Stop running all over the place, caught up in every activity possible, and run into the arms of grace. Run back to the Lover of your soul. Let Him embrace you and shower you with His love again. Let Him show you why you fell in love with Him in the first place. Be still.

REDO. In golf, it's called a mulligan. In video games, it's called a reset. Sometimes it's called a do-over. Simply put, start over again, doing it right this time. The word "first" (in v. 5) means "first in rank or importance."[7] Remember Jesus' primary command? Love God. How do you love God? Spend time with Him in His Word. Listen to Him. Be in authentic relationships with other believers who can remind you about the importance of your first love with Jesus.

Reflect

In today's reflection, record your thoughts as you have opportunity to remember, repent, and redo.

Remember   **Repent**   **Redo**

Respond

How did God speak to you today?

What is your response to Him?

week 2

quitting the family busyness

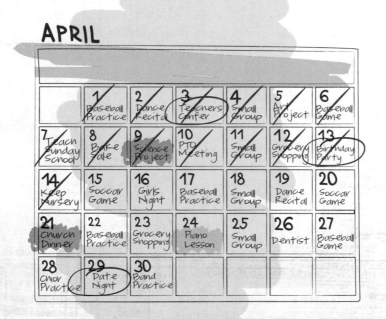

APRIL

	1 Baseball Practice	2 Dance Recital	3 Teachers Confer	4 Small Group	5 Art Project	6 Baseball Game
7 Teach Sunday School	8 Bake Sale	9 Science Project	10 PTO Meeting	11 Small Group	12 Grocery Shopping	13 Birthday Party
14 Keep Nursery	15 Soccar Game	16 Girls Night	17 Baseball Practice	18 Small Group	19 Dance Recital	20 Soccar Game
21 Church Dinner	22 Baseball Practice	23 Grocery Shopping	24 Piano Lesson	25 Small Group	26 Dentist	27 Baseball Game
28 Choir Practice	29 Date Night	30 Band Practice				

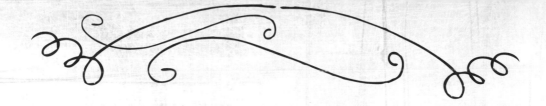

"It is not enough to be industrious; so are the ants. What are you industrious about?"

Henry David Thoreau

Do not be conformed to this world, but be transformed by the renewal of your mind, that by testing you may discern what is the will of God, what is good and acceptable and perfect. Romans 12:2, ESV

But the Lord answered her, "Martha, Martha, you are anxious and troubled about many things, but one thing is necessary. Mary has chosen the good portion, which will not be taken away from her." Luke 10:41-42, ESV

DVD session 2

Today's group: Carrie Betzen, Shelly Gleason, Kati Smith, Tami Overhauser

The _____ of busyness

Psalm 37:7: "Be still before the LORD and wait patiently for him."

"Be still" = **dâmam**; to *be* _____ , *to stop*; hold peace, quiet self, rest, be silent

When was the last time you were astonished by God?

We need to build a _____ _____ into our day, a time when we reflect on His goodness, love, and mercy. We are to be mindful of Him throughout the day.

QUESTION: Is it hard for you to be still before God? If so, what hinders you?

Psalm 23

"shepherd" = **râ'âh:** to *associate* with (as a friend); keep company with.

You _____ _____ _____ ____ _____ to God and be still.

We suffer from _____ = _____ _____ _____ .

QUESTION: In what areas of your life do you find yourself commonly distracted and overwhelmed with too much information or too many choices?

We have to ask ourselves, has this possession or choice _____ us?

Psalm 23:2: "Still" or "quiet waters" is a sharp contrast to the noise of the world.

Did David trade still waters for the busyness of life? It happens over time, and we are weakened and _____ ____ _____ .

Busyness is a _____ .

Hebrew meaning of "restores" = shûwb (*shoob*); bring (again, back, home again), carry again (back), continually, convert, deliver (again), draw back, fetch home again, go again (back, home), recover, refresh, relieve, render (again), rescue, restore, retrieve, (cause or make to) return.

Many of us are tired, weary, and in need of restoration. We want to walk with Him beside the still waters, but it requires action to _____ ____ _____ and eliminate things that are just not necessary.

Discuss together

How do you know when you need to get alone with the Lord?

Which meaning of "restores" most addresses your need right now?

"I like Cinderella, I really do. She has a good work ethic. I appreciate a good, hard-working gal. And she likes shoes."
Giselle in *Enchanted*

Downloads of this session are available at *www.lifeway.com*.

Day 1

Finding Your Happy Place

Mark 1:29-39; Mark 14:32-36

Have you ever had one of those days when you thought you might collapse from the load? I've had plenty that would qualify, but one in particular comes to mind and won't soon be forgotten. It actually fell on my twentieth wedding anniversary and has since been dubbed "the day from hell." Here's a summary of how that day played out:

• It was my grandfather's funeral and I was giving a short message at the service. My grandparents had a huge impact on my decision to become a Christian in my college years, so I was emotionally distraught over the loss.

• My Yorkie (5 months old at the time and weighing just 2 pounds) had jumped off the top of the sofa the day before and broken both front legs. His legs were splinted and surgery was scheduled the morning of my grandfather's funeral … 30 minutes from my home.

• A dear friend (who was to attend the funeral) had just completed a 30-day rehab program, only to fall off the wagon and go missing. I spent the day frantically trying to reach this person. All is well with this friend today, but May 23, 2007, was a different story.

• One family member had a car accident going into town on the morning of the funeral. It wasn't serious, but demanded attention.

I was literally pulled in every direction. Emotionally. Physically. Spiritually. I was spent before the day ever began. I made it through the day and I survived. Barely. By the end of the day, I just wanted to be alone with God. To talk to Him. Cry with Him. And beg Him to send me to rehab!

Why does it take difficult days to remind us of the importance of being alone with God? Should we not long for His company every day?

Let's go to rehab this week and work this problem out.

Recall

What are you like when you have not had much time alone and you need it?

How do you know when you need to get away with the Lord? What are the clues?

Do you ever feel guilty for taking time to be alone? Or for spending time with God when there is so much "serving" to be done? Explain.

Read

Last week, we focused on Jesus as the core and center of our lives, the One who will fulfill us and make us complete. However, for most of us, time away with the Lover of our souls feels more like a luxury than a priority. The demands of the day press in. Sometimes it's hard to take time away to be with God when the laundry is staring at you and the dishes are screaming to be washed, dried, and put away. Or at least loaded into the dishwasher.

I think God understands the pressure we feel. I think that's why He allowed the Gospel writers to glimpse Jesus' private life with the Father.

Read Mark 1:29-39.

What stands out to you about Jesus as you read these verses?

What stands out to you about the circumstances Mark described?

Describe the kinds of things Jesus did.

Put yourself in Jesus' sandals, so to speak.

How do you think Jesus' interactions with these people affected Him? Explain your answer.

Why do you think Jesus got up "very early in the morning, while it was still dark" (v. 35)?

How would you have responded to the comment of Simon's friends when they were looking for Him (v. 37)?

The Book of Mark is the shortest of the Gospels, but it moves like an action movie. It begins with John the Baptist's ministry and Jesus' baptism, moves straight into His wilderness experience, and, by chapter 1 verse 14, we are reading about the launch of His ministry.

The word "immediately" is used in Mark's Gospel twelve times in the New International Version, seventeen times in the King James Version, and a whopping forty times in the New American Standard Bible. Clearly, Jesus was on the move. He was a man driven to fulfill His assigned mission.

Mark 1 demonstrates Jesus' level of activity. In that chapter, He called His first disciples (vv. 16-20), drove out unclean spirits (vv. 21-27), and healed Peter's mother-in-law (vv. 29-31). That was just during the daylight hours. Mark records that "when evening came" (v. 32), the disciples brought Jesus the sick and demon-possessed. The entire town congregated at His doorstep (v. 33).

Now lest you think to yourself, *Of course Jesus could do all of this—He was God!* let me remind you of one important fact: Jesus was also 100 percent human. He was born in a stable to two scared-out-of-their-mind, faithful Jews. He went through adolescence just like we did. He was tempted by Satan just as we are. He was prone to exhaustion just like you and me. And yet, He recognized one important fact of His humanity: He knew He desperately needed time away with His Father.

I love how the King James Version renders verse 35: "And in the morning, rising up a great while before day, he went out, and departed into a solitary place, and there prayed."

There are a couple of words worth noting. First is the word "morning." Now that word could mean any time before noon. But, when you look at the Greek translation of morning, you find the word **prói**, which can be translated as "the fourth watch of the night."[1] Translation (get ready for it): between 3:00 and 6:00 in the morning! And just to give us a more definitive time, Mark added the phrase "while it was still dark." In the King James Version, it reads "a great while before day." The word "great" actually means "exceedingly beyond measure."[2]

"Exceedingly beyond measure" before day, combined with the "fourth watch" tells me that Jesus didn't get a whole lot of sleep that night! While everyone else was still deep in REM sleep, Jesus was sneaking off to be with His Father.

This is not a legalistic call for you to get up at 3:30 in the morning to have your quiet time. Goodness knows, I would be sleepwalking through my devotional.

What I am saying is this: if the Son of God needed time away with the Lord, you and I do too. I don't care when you take the time—afternoon, while the kids nap, or exceedingly before morning—just make space for the Lover of your soul to speak over you. You need it. So did Jesus.

Let's look at one other story that shows Jesus' need for communion with the Father. Read Mark 14:32-36.

Set the stage. What's going on in these verses?

Who accompanied Jesus?

What did Jesus tell His companions? Why is that significant?

What unusual thing did Jesus do (v. 35)? Why do you think He did that?

The scene Mark describes is one of the most moving accounts of Jesus with His friends. The night before the most gut-wrenching day in eternity, Jesus took His closest friends with Him into the garden of Gethsemane. Scripture records that Jesus began to be "deeply distressed and horrified" and poured out His heart to His closest friends (vv. 33-35).

And then what does Jesus do? He leaves them and falls to the ground in earnest, agonizing prayer. Now, you and I probably wouldn't have done that. As women, we would have grabbed the tissues, cried together, and tried to figure out a solution over coffee and chocolate. Women share sorrows together. We want someone to walk with us, to pray with us. To cry with us.

Jesus didn't take His companions with Him as "He went a little farther." Why? Was it a guy thing? I don't think so. It was a God thing. Jesus needed the companionship that only God can provide. Jesus understood that the *one* thing that would sustain Him over the next twenty-four hours was communion and union with His Father.

In the biggest trials of His life, Jesus turned to His Father. You and I have a lot to learn from Him.

Reflect

What things have you substituted for your time alone with the Father?

On whom do you rely to give you strength and peace instead of your Heavenly Father?

Respond

How did God speak to you today?

What is your response to Him?

Day 2

A Mary Pace in a Martha Race

Luke 10:38-42

In 2005 I was on a plane and headed to an event in Midland, Texas.
I remember it like it was yesterday because I didn't want to go.
Spiritually, I was on empty.

I was drowning in a sea of deadlines, speaking engagements, and mother/daughter
events my ministry was hosting throughout the country. My tendency to over-
commit had finally caught up with me, and I felt like I had nothing left to give.

Mind you, all the things I had overcommitted to were good things. God things. Or
were they? The truth is, God doesn't endorse a pace that leaves you with little to
no time for Him. Even if those things are eternal.

I sat on that plane with tear-filled eyes, wondering how I would find the strength
to step up on the stage and give the listeners Jesus when I desperately needed
Him myself. Perhaps most ironic was that I was giving a message based on the
passage we will study today. It's a passage that God continues to bring me back to
when I need a gentle reminder about keeping a healthy balance in ministry.

I made it through the event, but only because I decided to be perfectly honest
with the women about my struggle. I shared that I had been personally convicted by the passage we were talking about. They weren't going to hear from
some know-it-all who had it all together when it comes to maintaining a balance
between doing and being.

It's true that healing cannot really begin until you can openly admit you have a
problem. Similar to the alcoholic standing up at her first AA meeting and saying,
"Hi. My name is _____ and I'm an alcoholic," we too must be willing to come
clean. So, here goes: "Hi. My name is Vicki and I'm an overcommitter. I can't say
no." Whew. That felt good. Thanks for being my support group today.

Recall

Can you recall a time when you were doing a lot of stuff for God, but it flat wore you out?

Journal about the situation and how it affected your relationship with God and others.

Read

As women, we're prone to be doers. We see a problem, we fix it. We see a need, we meet it. One of your kids calls from school to say he forgot his football cleats? We're on it. A young woman at church just gave birth to her firstborn? The casseroles are on the way (or takeout, if I'm in charge).

That nurturing gene in us just cannot *not* respond when a need presents itself. But in the process of meeting others' needs, we forget that, sometimes, the greater need lies within us.

Read Luke 10:38-42. Before you do, take a second to ask God to allow you to read it with a fresh perspective.

Who welcomed Jesus into her home?

How do these verses describe her?

How do these verses describe her sister?

What was Martha's request of Jesus? What do you think she expected Him to say to Mary? How did Jesus actually respond?

How would you have felt if you were Martha?

It's interesting that Martha was the one who invited Jesus into her home, and yet she was the one who was "worried and upset about many things." I wonder how differently things might have gone had they gone to the local Starbucks or hung out at one of the disciples' homes. How many times have you *not* offered to host a Bible study or fellowship in your home because you knew what that meant? Straightening up the living room. Cleaning the bathroom. Putting away the dishes in the sink. Baking a snack or dessert. Burn candles three days prior to mask the sweaty teenage-boy smell. What a mess.

I imagine that's what was going on in Martha's head. The Messiah is in her living room. I would want everything to be just right for Him too. In all fairness to Martha, I think her heart was in the right place. She wanted to serve her Master. She wanted to prepare the food for Him and get the table set for Him.

But in so doing, she "was distracted" (v. 40). The King James Version says that Martha was "cumbered about much serving." Funny. The word "cumbered" means "to be driven about mentally; to be over-occupied, too busy, about a thing."[3] In other words, Martha became so over-occupied about serving Jesus that she forgot to listen to Him.

Caught up in the bustle of service, Martha lost perspective and actually accused Jesus of not caring about her situation. Wow. That's some *chutzpah*. And in her boldness, she actually told Jesus what to do: "Tell my sister to get back here in the kitchen and give me a hand with dinner."

Now before you condemn Martha and declare her to be the enemy (along with her namesake, Ms. Stewart), take a minute to do some introspection. You might find that you have a few of her genes. How often does your action and service get in the way of sitting at the feet of Jesus? Have you ever lost perspective? Have you ever told the Lord (or at least thought), "Look, I'm doing all I can for You, and You don't seem to be aware of the situation. I thought You loved me!?" Guilty.

The Master Teacher used this encounter as a teachable moment. "Martha, you're too distracted by stuff that doesn't matter right now. Some things are more important. Mary figured that out and I'm not going to chastise her for it." Ouch. Enough said.

So does this story teach us that service is unnecessary? That we should all just hang out in the sanctuary, read our Bibles, and wait for Jesus to speak (and the other Marthas to step up and serve)? No. Service is part of the Christian life. But service should be an outflow of our ongoing relationship with Jesus, not a replacement for it. Reread that last sentence and think about it.

If you're spending more time doing things for God than you are spending time with God, then something is out of whack. Sitting at Jesus' feet should always precede serving in His name. Always.

Now before you pack up your flannelgraph and resign from teaching Sunday School, let me offer this caveat: it's not about making sure everything equals out each week—two hours at church must equal two hours in the Bible. I think this passage is a reminder about rhythm, not balance.

Balance is a buzzword in our culture. Balanced diet. Balanced family life. Balanced church life. I see lots of blogs, books, and articles that give you tips on balancing life as a mom, wife, and career woman. While balance has its virtues, life may be as much about rhythm as about balance.

Notice that God created the world with four seasons—all filled with a variety of motion but also with dormancy. Without winter, there is no spring. Observe your body. It works best in rhythm—a period of rest followed by a period of activity followed by rest again. Remember the passage in Ecclesiastes 3? There is a season for everything—a time to dance and a time to refrain from dancing.

The key is to recognize those dormant periods and to take time to refuel and refocus when slow moments come. The key is taking advantage of the quiet moments—however they present themselves. On some days (or weeks), you may have a lot of time to give to your relationship with Jesus. On yet other days, your dormant period may come in the shower, and that's only if the kids cannot yell at you through the door. That's OK.

This story is a good reminder that just because you see a need doesn't necessarily mean that you need to meet it, or that you need to meet it immediately.

Serving can wait. Worship cannot.

Reflect

How have you been like Martha?

What are your primary distractions in the course of a day?

What would Jesus say to you today in your kitchen, office, or classroom?

Respond

How did God speak to you today?

What is your response to Him?

Day 3

When Religion Gets in the Way

Matthew 23:23-28

I don't have much patience with nitpickers. Take, for example, the woman who wanted to talk to me after a message (on how believers can focus more on rules than on redemption) I had shared at a women's event.

In an effort to move us beyond our Christian comfort zone of black-and-white thinking, I had encouraged the group to reflect on past sin and, more important, on moments when they had found themselves desperately in need of God's grace.

As you can imagine, it tugged on the heart of many women who were still struggling to accept God's forgiveness for things in their past. It challenged those who had become stale in their faith, forgetting the impact of the cross. I prayed with many of these women as they shared their stories.

And then I was approached by the nitpicker. She stood in line—not for prayer, not to share her story, but to inform me—get ready for it—that she had studied Greek in seminary and I had "mispronounced a couple of Greek words" when I was unpacking several key Scriptures.

Seriously? Is that all she got out of the entire message? I thanked her for her comment and told her I would take it under advisement.

I stewed about her nitpicky comment in the days that followed and took it before God's throne to ask Him what He wanted me to glean from it (as is my practice with any criticism). For the record, He didn't leave me with a charge to sign up for Greek at a nearby seminary. Actually, that would have been far less painful. Instead, He gently reminded me that I too have been the nitpicker on plenty of occasions. Ow.

Recall

Have you ever had a similar experience when God broke through your nitpicky, self-righteous views? Describe the circumstances.

Read

When we nitpick, we get concerned with insignificant details. Like the time I complained to someone on our church staff that the air conditioner was way too cold. Ugh. Or the time I attended an event with a friend and critiqued the cheesy drama sketch after it was over. Am I any different from the woman who approached me to nitpick over my inability to speak fluent Greek? Busted.

Why do Christians get so caught up in nitpicking over insignificant details that don't matter one iota in the scheme of eternity? When I think back on my own habit of nitpicking, it flourished at a time in my life when I had grown calloused to God's nudgings in my heart. It was easier (and less painful) to point out the faults of others rather than take a deep look within.

Believe it or not, this spiritual nitpicking problem has been around since Jesus' day (and longer), according to Old Testament prophets.

Read Matthew 23:23-28.

Who was Jesus addressing in these verses?

How does Jesus describe them? List the nicknames He gave them.

What terms did Jesus use to illustrate the condition of their hearts?

Why do you think Jesus was so harsh toward these people?

Wow. The Prince of peace sure knows how to stir up trouble with the scribes and Pharisees. No wonder these religious leaders wanted to kill Jesus. So why was Jesus so harsh? A little background will help answer that question.

In Old Testament times, the Jews believed in the Torah, or the written law that God gave to the Israelites as the first five books of the Bible. The Jews also believed in the oral law—an explanation of the written law—which was written down during the Babylonian exile. This was called the Mishnah. Eventually, the rabbis and scholars wrote commentaries on the Mishnah, and these commentaries were called the Gemara. Together, the Mishnah and the Gemara made up the Talmud. Following so far?

By the time Jesus was born, the commands of God in the Old Testament had been expanded. A good Jew would follow not only the Torah, or the Old Testament, but also everything in the Mishnah. That meant following 613 commandments.

The Pharisees believed in strict adherence to all Jewish law and tradition—even to the most mundane activities. They were considered expert and accurate inter- preters of Jewish law. And they followed all 613 laws. To. The. Letter.

Why was Jesus so ticked off at the religious leaders like the Pharisees? Because the Pharisees—experts in Scripture—were actually using Scripture to browbeat God's people into what they thought a good Jewish person should look like. God doesn't like it when His Word gets twisted, especially when it creates a barrier between Him and the people He loves.

Unfortunately, people are still using Scripture in God's name to browbeat others, weighing them down and drawing them away from God instead of toward Him. And if we're not careful, you and I can become one of those people.

How? When we are so busy acting like Jesus that we forget to love Him. When we're so busy applying God's Word that we forget to read it. When we're so busy defending one portion of Scripture that we forget the whole counsel of God's Word. When we're so convinced that our interpretation of Scripture is right that we don't allow the Holy Spirit to tell us what God wants to communicate.

Let me meddle just a minute: Has your work for God replaced your worship of Him? Has religious adherence to Scripture replaced your relationship with God? Are you so busy making sure everybody knows how much you do at church that you've lost track of the broken condition of your heart?

That's what had happened to the Pharisees. They were so focused on doing the right thing for so long that they forgot why they were doing it in the first place. They lost track of their heart and, in the absence of a growing walk with God, legalism stepped in and filled the void. Doing took the place of being. Service replaced servanthood. Work replaced worship and wonder. Lists replaced love.

Jesus was so popular with the people because He took the weight of the law off their shoulders. He blew fresh wind into their faith. He gave them room to breathe, to try again, to hope that perhaps God really did love them even though they were imperfect. He showed them what love could do in the absence of legalism. Maybe you need to ask Jesus to do the same for you.

Perhaps you've been so weighed down by religious activity that you've lost your love relationship with Jesus. Remember, Jesus wants your heart. He died so that you could have a relationship with Him, not so that you could bake another casserole, sign up for another class, or serve on yet another committee.

He loves *you*, not what you do for Him.

Reflect

How would you describe the condition of your heart?

How has activity replace the awe and wonder of knowing Jesus?

Respond

How did God speak to you today?

What is your response to Him?

Day 4

Rest Stop Ahead

Psalm 46:10-11; Matthew 11:28-30

I have the wonderful privilege of watching my grandson one day a week. When he was an infant, it was a piece of cake. (Well, except for the time I had to install a car seat and nearly lost my sanity in the process.) Recently, he began to walk, and everything changed. The world he stared at for months on end is finally within his reach.

On a recent overnight visit, he was literally on the move from sunup to sundown, minus a one-hour afternoon nap. At one point, I tried to sit down and check my email while he was playing busily with a crate of toys. Minutes later, I heard him in the next room chattering happily while dumping the dog food out of the dog's bowl. And minutes after that (while I'm cleaning up the dog food!), he managed to locate the only cabinet in the kitchen that doesn't have a safety latch on it and yanked out Tupperware bowls and lids at warp speed.

At that point, I decided it would be a good break (and diversion) to take him to the neighborhood park down the street. Once at the park, he zigzagged from the swings to the slide to the sandbox, and back to the swings again, all within ten minutes. When we got home, it was more of the same: he explored and I followed.

That evening, we prepared for bedtime and a strange thing happened. He finally began to wind down. He was exhausted. He has never been much of a snuggler and typically squirms out of my lap the minute I pick him up, but not tonight. He sat perfectly still in my lap while we read two books. When I picked him up to put him in the crib, he laid his head on my shoulder. When I got to the crib, I just couldn't bring myself to lay him down.

I stood there for what must have been about five minutes and swayed that baby gently in my arms. I prayed for him. Sang over him. And I even stole a few kisses from his chubby cheeks. I didn't know when (or if) I'd get another moment where he would be perfectly still in my arms, so I took full advantage of the opportunity. As I placed him in the crib, I wondered if that's what it's like for God when we move busily through our days, consumed with the world's ongoing noise.

When was the last time you slowed down long enough to crawl up in the Father's lap and let Him sing over you?

Recall

Think about a time when you felt like you were running in all directions, unable to catch your breath. What was that like?

What happens to you when you are too busy? How does busyness affect you physically? Emotionally? Spiritually? Socially?

Read

As women, we pride ourselves on our skills at multitasking. Sure, I can cook supper, help the kids with their homework, start a load of laundry, and listen to my husband as he shares about his day. No worries! How many times have you juggled more than one project at home, school, or the office? The pressure to spin more plates has been multiplied by the emergence and proliferation of technology.

Everything goes faster, so we should keep up. The frenzy to stay "on"—connected, working, doing—is rampant. And it is killing us slowly. Consider this commentary from a tech website, of all places:

> Americans for centuries have believed that new labor saving devices will free us from the burdens of the workplace and give us more time to ponder philosophy, goof off, explore the arts, and hang around with friends and family.

> So here we are at the start of the 21st century, enjoying one of the greatest technological boom times in human history, and nothing could be further from the truth.

The very tools that were supposed to liberate us have bound us to our work (and schools) in ways that were inconceivable just a few years ago. But technology almost never does what we expect.

Almost all of us, especially the people reading this, have less leisure time than ever before. We work harder, take fewer vacations for shorter periods of time, report more stress than almost any other demographic group, and find the boundaries between work and play increasingly blurred. Computing and communications technologies are eroding our privacy and leisure.[4]

Now, guess when this article was written: 2000. Over a decade has gone by and we haven't slowed down a bit. The boundaries between work and play are even weaker, given that we are even busier. We're supposedly more productive than ever before, but at what cost?

The Centers for Disease Control tell us that the lack of sleep (from extended computing and media time) makes us more likely "to suffer from chronic diseases such as hypertension, diabetes, depression, and obesity, as well as from cancer, increased mortality, and reduced quality of life and productivity."[5] One thing the researchers didn't mention is the toll it takes on your family and friends, plus your relationship with God.

That's one of the reasons God instituted the Sabbath, so that we would stop doing long enough to catch our breath and get perspective on all of those "important" tasks we're busting ourselves to complete.

Read Psalm 46:10-11 slowly. Don't read it like a newspaper article or blog post. Sit with it a minute. Let it marinate in your soul a bit. Then move on to answer the questions.

What is the command in verse 10?

According to these verses, who is in ultimate control?

How do these verses describe the One who is control? What phrases are used?

Psalm 46:10 is a powerful verse, no matter what translation you use.

- "Be still, and know that I am God" (NIV, New Living Translation, ESV, KJV, American Standard Version).

- "Cease striving and know that I am God" (NASB).

- "Stop your fighting—and know that I am God" (HCSB).

- "Be in awe and know that I am God" (International Standard Version).

- "Let go of your concerns! Then you will know that I am God" (God's Word Translation).

- "Desist, and know that I [am] God" (Young's Literal Translation).

Do you get the point? STOP! SIT STILL! How many times have you said to a child, "Stop running around! Get in your seat and stay there! Stop jumping up and down! Get down from the table and come sit beside me! Be still!"

Sometimes I picture God like that parent, telling His children to calm down long enough to climb up into His lap and enjoy His company. But like petulant children, we run around like a bunch of whirling banshees, too preoccupied with our games to listen to what He has to say.

Why is it so difficult for us to sit still? Why do we feel better when we are doing? I think the answer to that question lies in the second part of verse 10: "know that I am God."

We think we're in control of things. We run a tight ship at home. Micromanage at work. Control the uncontrollable. Makes us feel safer, stronger, more valuable. Indispensable. Needed.

Reality check, ladies: you are not God. Neither am I. Even though we think we would do a better job of running the White House, the company, or even the church, I can tell you unequivocally that God is Sovereign over all the earth. You won't do a better job than He does.

Be honest: how would you describe your emotional and mental state right now? If I polled the people in my Sunday School class, I would hear responses like *exhausted, overwhelmed, overworked, weary, worn out, swamped, defeated, deflated, discouraged, disillusioned*.

Why? Because we don't take time to be still. Because we're too busy trying to run the universe instead of relying on the Lord of hosts (v. 11). Instead of remembering that the God of Jacob is the source of our strength, we rely on ourselves.

And the end result? Exhaustion.

Now, before you berate yourself, let me assure you that you are not the only one who struggles with being still, who wrestles with the demon of doing. In fact, Jesus Himself addressed it. Listen to what He has to say.

> Read Matthew 11:28-30 in The Message slowly, taking in the emotion and heartfelt plea of your Savior:

"Are you tired? Worn out? Burned out on religion? Come to me. Get away with me and you'll recover your life. I'll show you how to take a real rest. Walk with me and work with me— watch how I do it. Learn the unforced rhythms of grace. I won't lay anything heavy or ill-fitting on you. Keep company with me and you'll learn to live freely and lightly."

Be honest. When you read those verses, did you think, "Where do I sign up?" We are tired. Worn out. Burned out on religion. We need real rest. We need to recover life as Jesus intended. We need to learn the unforced rhythms of grace to overcome the tyranny of the urgent.

The truth is, Jesus didn't save you so you would get burned out. That abundant life that He promised was supposed to be in *this* lifetime, not just the next. But the key to that abundant life is in verse 28: "Come to me. Get away with me."

Be still. Whatever that means for you—taking five minutes to sit in your favorite chair while the kids are at school or taking a nap—take the time to be still.

Reflect

Do you struggle with being still?

If so, what do you think the Father would say to you if you were still enough to hear it?

Respond

How did God speak to you today?

What is your response to Him?

There is power in being still. Sometimes God can't speak to us, minister to us, or do what He wants to do in our lives because we cannot sit still long enough to hear and obey Him. Evaluate why you are unwilling to sit still. Also note that in Psalm 46:10-11, He *will* be exalted among the nations and the earth.

His being exalted has nothing to do with our working or exalting Him. His exaltation is a given with or without our activity.

Day 5

Missing God in the Midst of Busy

Isaiah 40:10-11

I have always felt closer to God when I'm outdoors. A few years ago, I began walking in my neighborhood. My goal was not only to get in better shape physically, but spiritually as well. I walk anywhere from one to three miles several days a week. Sometimes, I put my earbuds in and listen to my worship playlist, but other times I unplug completely and appreciate the silence.

Even though I'm technically in motion, it has become a time of stillness for me before God. I pray. I worship. I praise. Sometimes, I even shed a tear of gratitude over His faithfulness in my life. I need the time to bring me back to the basics. To remind me that He is God and I'm not. To be silent and hear Him speak.

I began walking during a difficult trial in my life. I found myself in a place where, once again, I was doubting God's love. Unfortunately, it's a place I find myself in more often than I care to admit. I can accept that He loves *you* unconditionally, but this concept of unconditional love has always been difficult for me to understand and, more important, receive for myself.

I have a lot of skeletons in my closet—some of which came after I became a Christian, when I should have known better. Walking helps me slow down and talk to God about my past mistakes, allowing Him to minister to my doubt, guilt, and shame. To remind me that I'm loved by a perfect God in spite of my imperfect track record.

On one walk in which I was dealing with shame and guilt, I was crying out to Him (silently, of course, lest I scare the neighbors) for a reminder of His love. And there, a few feet in front of me, I saw it: a beautiful heart-shaped rock. I picked it up and wept. It was just the reminder I needed in that moment to get me through the day. To replace the lie the enemy had tried so hard to get me to believe—that my sin was far too big for the unconditional love of Christ.

I brought that heart-shaped rock home and put it in a glass jar on a shelf in my office to remind me that He loves me even when I'm not particularly lovable.

Today that jar is filled to the brim with heart-shaped rocks found on my many walks. I'm well on my way to filling up another jar that sits next to the original jar on my shelf.

I can't help but smile when I see the jars. Every single rock is a reminder that I am loved by the Father. No matter what. I imagine He'll keep on placing them in my path until I get the message.

Recall

Can you think of a time when God reminded you of His love?

What in your life could use God's healing touch or direction today?

Read

Sitting still before God has become a luxury in today's economy of time. So I'm going to help you out. Today's Bible study won't be study. The time you would normally spend reading and writing and thinking will instead be spent in stillness.

If you've never tried this spiritual discipline, that's OK. I'll walk you through it. The goal is to spend one hour with Him.

Keep in mind that you are likely to feel a myriad of emotions as you come to sit before God: anticipation, anxiety, anger, excitement, fear of the unknown, uneasiness. Whatever you feel is OK. Just tell God. You can say something like, "God, I want to spend this time with You, but I feel _____ because _____."

He knows and understands. Just don't let what you feel create a barrier between you and Jesus. That's what the enemy wants. Instead, allow your emotions to draw you closer to Him by being honest with Him about those feelings.

Find a quiet place, free from distractions and noise—even music. Take a few deep breaths, allowing your body to relax.

Thank God that He is present with you, even if you cannot sense Him. He wants to spend time with You. He is thrilled that you have taken time to be with Him.

Read Isaiah 40:10-11. Read it through three times. Read it aloud if possible. Read it slowly and allow it to soak in. When you come to a word or a phrase that catches your attention, stop there.

Ask God what He wants to say to you through those words. Wait for Him to respond. When you sense a nudge from the Holy Spirit, move on to the next portion of the passage.

Repeat this process, reading slowly and pausing when words or phrases catch your attention. Think of this time as the opportunity to soak in the Scripture, to allow its truths to sink below the surface of your intellect into the very marrow of your soul.

After you have read the Scripture three times, reflect and meditate on the portions of Scripture that God pointed out to you. Ask Him again to speak to you about what you have read. At the end of your time together, simply write down how God spoke to you.

We have provided plenty of space for you to write about your experience. Once you are finished, thank God for meeting with you and for speaking to you. Thank Him for the deep love He holds for you.

Respond

How did God speak to you today?

What is your response to Him?

Know that I am praying for you as you engage in these special times with the Father. Can you imagine what would happen if you devoted even *more* uninterrupted time to enjoying and listening to God? He covets daily intimacy with you, and being still before the Lord can mark all of your times with Him.

week 3

marriage matters

"Not all girls want Prince Charming and happily ever after. Some just want a man who is willing to stand by her side and ride the wave through the storm with her."

Unknown

And be kind and compassionate to one another, forgiving one another, just as God also forgave you in Christ.

Ephesians 4:32

DVD session 3

Today's group: Carrie Betzen, Tami Overhauser, Jaclyn Benson, Anna Jenkins

QUESTION: When did you experience Prince-Charming letdown?

Themes of romance films
> First love—All ends well when heroine returns to first love
> Obsessive love—Self-explanatory
> Courage of love—Taking a risk
> Downstairs Woman and Upstairs Man—Out of reach

"We maintain the fantasy that if we find our one true soul mate, everything wrong with us will be healed. No lover, no human being, is qualified for that role. No one can live up to that. The inevitable result is bitter disillusionment."—Tim Keller, *Counterfeit Gods*

Our culture has made an _____ out of the wedding day and a _____ out of marriage.

QUESTION: Was there a time you bought into the idea that one true soul mate would come along and heal your past, your hurts, and everything that's wrong with you?

What a man desires is _____ _____ .

Proverbs 19:22

We have _____ the part of the prince.

Ephesians 3:14-19

"filled" = plēroō (play-rŏ´-o): to cram, or level up a hollow

"God didn't put a parent and a child in the Garden, but a husband and a wife."
Tim Keller, *The Meaning of Marriage*

"(My husband and I) have a standing weekly date—Saturday morning breakfasts. Every Saturday my husband gets up and makes ME breakfast! As we eat together, we talk and get all caught up on each other's week and dream about the future together. Our breakfasts often last two hours (or more) as we sit together just chatting and sipping coffee. It truly is my favorite 'date.'"
Robin, married 29 years, in *Ever After*

Discuss together

What shared adventure has God set forth for you and your husband? How is it going?

What kind of dates do you and your husband plan to keep your marriage strong and vibrant?

Downloads of this session are available at *www.lifeway.com*. *Bonus: Check out segments from Carrie and Jaclyn related to their marriage struggles and joys.*

Day 1

Playing for Keeps

Genesis 2:18-25

While going though a box of old photos from my mother, I found a
picture of myself and some neighborhood kids playing "house" under
a patio table covered by sheets. I was probably three or four years old,
but it was clear that I was the matriarch of that makeshift table castle.

I had one of my mother's purses slung over my shoulder and wore a pair of
dress-up high heels as I hoisted a baby doll on my hip. A neighbor boy with an
indignant expression stood beside me in the picture. It was clear he had been
recruited to play the bread-winning patriarch and was none too happy about it. My
mother told me I even made the poor fellow kiss me shortly after the picture was
snapped—right before I shooed him off to his pretend job.

Many of us grew up with an idea that marriage was little more than grown-ups
playing house. Influenced by a combination of factors, we either view marriage as
something positive or negative. Most of us walk into the first year of marriage with
unrealistic expectations and are caught off guard when the newlywed buzz wears
off. Few of us had parents who took the time to teach us about the origins of
marriage and, more important, God's purpose for marriage. Marriage is hard, but
worth all the effort.

Recall

When you were a child, how did you picture marriage? Was your
impression positive or negative?

What influenced your view of marriage when you were growing up?

How is your picture of marriage different now?

Read

Peruse any self-help aisle in a bookstore and you'll see countless books on relationships and marriage. Even in Christian bookstores, the shelves are crammed with books on the secret to a happy and fulfilling relationship with your spouse. Go to a marriage conference and you'll get even more advice—some helpful and some not so much.

But what does Scripture tell us about marriage? To quote Julie Andrews in *The Sound of Music*, let's start at the very beginning, a very good place to start—in the Book of Genesis.

Read Genesis 2:18-25.
Why did God create marriage?

What did God say about Adam being alone?

What did God say He would do about Adam's solitude?

How did God help Adam to see that it wasn't good for him to be alone?

How did God create Eve? How was that different from how He created Adam? Why is that significant?

What was Adam's response to God giving him Eve?

If you've spent any time in church, you have probably read these verses or heard sermons on the passage—maybe even had it read at your own wedding. Sometimes familiarity with a Scripture leads to boredom, even apathy. Don't slip into that mode as we discover what marriage was intended to be.

In verse 18, God said, "It is not good for the man to be alone." Think back over the creation story. Every time God created something, He said, "It is good." This is the first time in the Bible that God said something was *not* good. Why? God saw that Adam needed something else—"a helper suitable for him" (v. 18, NIV).

Now before you roll your eyes, thinking this will be another sermon on helping your husband, hang on. God didn't create Eve because Adam needed a helper to make the casseroles and remember to send birthday cards to family members. The word "helper" is much stronger than that.

In Hebrew, the word "helper" is *ezer*. In the Old Testament, it is used approximately twenty more times after the Genesis references—overwhelmingly in reference to God. In fact, one of the names of God is Jehovah Ezer (the Lord Our Help; Ps. 33:20).[1]

Check out a few of these other references:

"Because he had said, 'The God of my father was my helper *[ezer]* and delivered me from Pharaoh's sword'" (Ex. 18:4).

"Blessed are you, Israel! Who is like you, a people saved by the LORD? He is your shield and helper *[ezer]* and your glorious sword" (Deut. 33:29, NIV).

"But as for me, I am poor and needy; come quickly to me, O God. You are my help *[ezer]* and my deliverer; LORD, do not delay" (Ps. 70:5, NIV).

"I lift up my eyes to the mountains—where does my help [ezer] come from? My help *[ezer]* comes from the LORD, the Maker of heaven and earth" (Ps. 121:1-2, NIV).

Look over those verses carefully. Notice the tone. These are not the writings of someone who needs help making supper or doing the laundry. These verses describe situations in which someone desperately needs God.

The point? Your husband desperately needs you. Your husband desperately needs you to come through for him. He wouldn't need you to come through for him if something important were not at stake. Now, I can't tell you what your husband needs you to do as his *ezer* because every man and every marriage is different. But I can tell you this: whatever God sets before you, He wants you to go through it in complete unity—in oneness of heart, spirit, and purpose.

Take a look at Genesis 2:24 (NIV): "That is why a man leaves his father and mother and is united to his wife, and they become one flesh." Yes, this is describing sex, but I think the meaning is much greater than just physical communion. Otherwise, why would He take a rib from Adam? Why wouldn't God just create Eve as He had created Adam—out of the dust of the earth? Because there's something shared between them. Her creation from Adam is a symbol of a shared life, a shared adventure.

If you are married, you know that marriage is an adventure. Doing life together is full of challenges and risks and dangers and unexpected turns. In the midst of all the craziness that life brings, there is an enemy who wants nothing less than the total destruction of your marriage and your individual lives as well. What better way to take down the Kingdom than to take out its warriors?

According to Genesis 1:28 (NIV), God set forth marriage as a union between a man and a woman as they fulfill God's plan for them.

"God blessed them and said to them, 'Be fruitful and increase in number; fill the earth and subdue it. Rule over the fish in the sea and the birds in the sky and over every living creature that moves on the ground.'"

Notice that God blessed them and, in essence, said to them, "The dominion of the earth is a joint project. You are to share in that adventure together." And while the fall changed the dynamics of the husband-wife relationship, God's intention for marriage remains. He still desires couples to walk together with Him, fulfilling His plans for them. What that looks like is different for every couple, but make no mistake: you are your husband's *ezer*, his come-alongside-and-fight-with-him warrior.

Don't settle for anything less. Your husband—and God's kingdom—need you.

Reflect

In what ways does your husband need you to be his *ezer*, the one he desperately needs?

What shared adventure has God set forth in your marriage?

How have you both settled for less than what God designed for marriage to be?

Respond

How did God speak to you today?

What is your response to Him?

Day 2

Save the Date

Genesis 1:26-31; 2:18-25; Ecclesiastes 4:9-12

When Keith and I married, we planned to wait several years before starting a family. Imagine our shock when fewer than four months into marriage, we discovered we were expecting. We celebrated our one-year anniversary at a Lamaze birthing class, and our son was born exactly thirteen months after our wedding.

By the time we celebrated our sixth anniversary, we had three children ages five and under. And by our seventh anniversary, we were sitting in a counselor's office with a marriage on life support.

Somewhere along the way, we had forgotten how to be husband and wife. The bulk of our time and energy was devoted to raising our three small children. We gained some valuable tools during our time in counseling, but one of the best pieces of advice we ever got was to reinstate the priority of making and keeping a date night. No exceptions.

From that point forward, rarely did two weeks go by that we didn't go on a date. Like most young couples, we were on a budget, so we swapped childcare with friends and looked for cost-saving, creative ways to spend time together. We caught up with each other and talked about things other than raising children. At first, it was hard to think of things to talk about since the bulk of our time revolved around taking care of our children. But before long, we were a couple again, laughing and enjoying each other's company, much like the days before we married and our kids arrived on the scene.

Twenty-six wedding anniversaries later, we are empty nesters who fully appreciate the value of those established date nights. We've watched many couples launch their last child from the nest only to discover they have nothing in common with each other. Somewhere along the way, they ceased being a couple, basing their identity on their children's academic pursuits and extracurricular activities. Some couples divorce, while many coexist as silent roommates.

When Keith and I dropped our last child off at college, it was bittersweet. We love being parents but, at the same time, we look forward to even more time with each other. We didn't face the awkward challenge of having to get reacquainted. We just picked right back up where we left off. Keith and I are living proof that saving the date can save the marriage.

Recall

When was the last time you and your husband went out on a date?

How do you feel when you haven't had alone time with your husband?

Read

You've heard the old adage that the only way you can grow in your relationship with God is to spend time with Him. That same principle applies to any relationship, but it is most significant when thinking about your marriage. If you and your husband don't spend time together, then your relationship will flounder. That time spent talking together, praying together, and, yes, sharing physical intimacy, does matter. Deeply.

However, the commitment to spend time together competes with other demands—work, parenting, church, community involvement, hobbies. In the end, something has to give. But God never intended for that to be your time with your spouse.

Read Genesis 1:26-31 and 2:18-25 through the lens of marriage.

From our study in day 1, what can you remember about the word "helper" and its significance in marriage?

What were Adam and Eve supposed to do, according to these verses?

What did God say after creating Adam and Eve as a couple?
(See Gen. 1:29-30.)

Who else is mentioned in these verses?

In these two chapters in Genesis, God creates Adam and Eve and, in doing so, established the first marriage. Notice that this marriage even preceded creation of the church. Before any other organization, institution, group, coalition, or committee, God created marriage. That tells us its importance. Marriage was not an afterthought, a spur-of-the-moment idea, or an addendum. God was purposeful in the union of man and woman.

Who isn't there? That's right—children. God created adults first. Children were a product of the marriage of Adam and Eve.

God put the couple in the garden sans children. Why do I bring up this point? Because a lot of couples sacrifice their time alone when children come along. Movie nights and outings often get replaced by school projects and late-night feedings. Play dates take the place of real dates. And then when the children get older, time previously spent together is filled by chauffeuring those children to hockey games, volleyball practice, art class, and, yes, even church.

Over time, that critical relationship between husband and wife begins to erode. Kissing becomes less frequent. You turn out the light and turn on the TV. Church committees and weekends at work drive a wedge between lovers. Best friends become strangers.

If you're like me (and others), the shift doesn't occur intentionally. It just happens over time, just as a leaf drifts downstream in the current. Without knowing it, a couple very much in love can drift along in the current of family and work and church and activities without realizing they have drifted apart in the process.

The distance between husband and wife can cause all sorts of problems. Infidelity. Arguments. Lack of communication. Assumptions. Unmet expectations. Jealousy. Addictions. And divorce.

So how do you know if you're in trouble? Let's talk.

Is your last date night with your husband (no kids!) a distant memory?

Do you talk more to your girlfriends or your husband about deep issues?

Are you more attached to an electronic gadget than to your husband?

Do you spend more time at church or in other activities than you spend with your husband?

Do you daydream about what your life would be like if you weren't married (or were married to someone else)?

If you answered yes to those questions, then you are treading dangerous waters. But do not despair. God wants you to succeed in your marriage more than you do.

Read Ecclesiastes 4:9-12. Pay close attention to verse 12.

"Two are better than one because they have a good reward for their efforts. For if either falls, his companion can lift him up; but pity the one who falls without another to lift him up. Also, if two lie down together, they can keep warm; but how can one person alone keep warm? And if someone overpowers one person, two can resist him. A cord of three strands is not easily broken."

So who is this third cord? It's not a child or a church member, and it's definitely not an in-law (no disrespect intended). The third presence? Almighty God. Only when a marriage is established and nurtured through an ongoing relationship with God can it survive the rigors and aggravations of life. Two people leave their families to create one of their own, but that union is held together by the sustaining, life-giving power of God.

What does that look like?

- Praying with and for each other.

- Participating in a small group that nurtures your marriage.

- Reading Scripture together and talking about what it means for each of you.

- Going on walks together and soaking in God's creation together.

- Playing together. Racing go-carts. Hiking in the mountains. Embarrassing yourselves in a Just Dance competition. Throwing a blanket on the front lawn and watching the stars after you tuck the kids into bed. Enjoying each other's company as your only agenda item.

Make no mistake: taking time for each other requires effort. It requires swimming against the stream of apathy, indifference, and the path of least resistance. Our culture surrounds us with quick marriages and quick divorces. To make your spouse and your marriage a priority requires work.

As Caitlin Flanagan noted in the July 2, 2009, *Time* magazine article "Is There Hope for the American Marriage?": "We recognize that it (lasting marriage) is something of great worth, but we are increasingly less willing to put in the hard work and personal sacrifice to get there."

If you are willing to spend the time and emotional effort to build and maintain your bond with your husband, you'll soon rediscover the joy of a stolen kiss, late-night pillow talk, and laughter together.

Reflect

On a scale of *1* to *10*, with *1* being weak and *10* being strong, how would you rate the current state of your marriage? Why?

What factors are contributing to weak areas in your marriage?

What can you do right now to strengthen your marriage?

Respond

How did God speak to you today?

What is your response to Him?

Day 3

Two Sides to Every Coin

Proverbs 6:6-8; 22:7; Luke 12:13-34

You have never met a more frugal man than my husband, Keith. Dave Ramsey often calls him for advice. OK, not really, but he should. When we first married, I found Keith's frugality to be endearing. That lasted about thirty days until we got into a huge rift over my buying a pair of black shoes.

He argued that I already owned a pair of black shoes (they were pumps). I explained that not all black shoes are created equal (the shoes in question were flats). He launched into a mini-sermonette on needs versus wants. I held my ground, boldly declaring that black flats are a nonnegotiable need. (Seriously, did the man expect me to wear my black pumps with my shorts during the summer?!)

And thus began our unhealthy pattern of dealing with money. In a nutshell, my husband is a saver and I am a spender. My husband operates under the philosophy of "Eat generic, drink water, and save everything, for you might just live forever." In truth, I am grateful I have a husband who takes his role as provider very seriously. His frugal ways have left us debt-free and financially secure at a time when many couples in our stage of life are scrambling to make ends meet. It took awhile, but we learned the art of compromise. Sometimes he gets his way and sometimes I get my way ... or black flats—whatever the case may be.

Recall

Compare your philosophy of spending and saving with your husband's. How are you alike and how are you different?

When was the last time you and your husband argued about money? What was the conflict about?

Read

Do a cursory search on the Internet for "causes of divorce" and you will find money at the top of the list. Financial matters are one of the major areas of conflict in marriages. Because opposites do attract in relationships, it's likely that one person is the spender and the other is the saver. These different approaches to money can seem cute or quirky while you're dating, but when you get married, those attitudes become a source of tension that wears down wedded bliss.

What does Scripture say about money, spending, debt, savings, IRAs, and 401(k)s?

Read Proverbs 6:6-8.
What is the subject of these verses?

What is the point of this proverb?

When you first read this proverb, what was your initial gut reaction?

If you're the saver in the family, you might be tempted to use these verses as ammunition against your husband's spending ways. If you like to spend, you probably grumbled the entire time you read this proverb. But the writer has a point, doesn't he? Without saving, there will be nothing for the harvest. I know you're thinking: "I don't live on a farm!" So let's translate for the twenty-first century.

Have you ever had something minor done to your car—like get the oil changed—only to be told that you need the alternating flux capacitor thingamabob fixed? And that it'll cost $42 million? Hello, harvest time. Or your doctor tells you you have myopic pharynx mitosis of the pancreas, which must be remedied by surgery, of which your insurance will only cover 70 percent? Yep, harvest time.

OK, so I've made you angry—or given you ammunition. What else does Scripture tell us?

Read Proverbs 22:7 (and don't get mad at me—I didn't write this).
What bit of wisdom do we learn here?

This verse is not very popular in our current take-it-home-today-but-pay-for-it-later economy. But the writer had a point.

How does the lender control you? By the monthly payment. Having to pay the MasterCard or Visa piper every month hinders you from doing what you would really like to do with that money. The more debt you incur, the more enslaved you will become.

Think about how you could spend your money if you didn't make payments on a house, car, or shoes (personal ouch!) that you had to have. What would you do with that money? Mission trip? Sponsor a child in Guatemala? Save up for a new refrigerator? You get the point.

Lest you think I'm picking on the spenders, let's look at the other side of the coin.

Read Luke 12:13-34.
On whom does this parable center?

What was the rich man's problem?

What would have corrected the problem?

What words of encouragement did Jesus offer about material possessions and treasure?

What did Jesus say about the Father's provisions?

Do you think these verses are an admonition against saving?

Why or why not?

What point do you think Jesus was trying to make here?

If people looked at your treasures, where would they say your heart is?

Obviously, Jesus wasn't telling His disciples to empty out their bank accounts. His teaching wasn't intended to cause the Jerusalem market to crash. What He was pointing out was this: watch out lest your heart be consumed by the stuff you own. Before long, it can become the focus of your life. It can take the place of God in your heart. The more stuff you own, the more stuff owns you—unless you are *very* careful to keep the right perspective.

And what is the right perspective? That you really don't own anything. It's all God's. Every bit of money you earn belongs to God. And the stuff you buy is transient. It can be gone in a flash, so don't set your heart on it. What's most important is God and His kingdom, not your own castle made of brick and mortar.

What the Bible teaches about money is balance. You save and you spend. You seek God's perspective on what you have and ask His direction on how to use it. Your house can be a noose around your neck or it can be a ministry tool. Your car can be a transport for kids who need a ride or it can be your "baby."

Now that we know more about what Scripture says about money, let's get practical. How do you talk with your husband about finances without yelling, throwing tantrums, or pouting? Here are a few suggestions:

1. Deal with your own demons. Why have you adopted your money style? Why are you a spender (or a saver)? For example, a friend and her husband struggled over saving versus spending. She grew up in a family that had very little money to spare. Dining out was a rarity. Shopping at K-Mart, not Stein Mart, was the only option.

   When she finally finished school and got a good job, she was thrilled at the loosening of the financial belt. She married a man whose mother was the vice president of a bank, and he had learned early on the importance of saving. Together, their approaches to money created the perfect storm of conflict. However, when she began to understand why she reacted so strongly to any mention of a budget, the conflicts lessened.

2. Pray together. It's really difficult to argue over money when you both agree that it's not yours in the first place. Ask God how you can advance His kingdom through your finances. When you seek God's direction, the focus shifts from your individual opinions to God's leadership. And that's a really good place to be.

3. Hear each other out. Rather than just assuming your spouse is wrong and you are right, stop for a minute and just listen. Listen with your ears and with your heart. What's going on with him? And what's driving this conflict?

4. Make a bucket list together. If you weren't in debt, what would you want to do together? Go on an Alaskan cruise? Add a room to the back of the house? Adopt a child from another country? Use that list as a motivating factor for how you spend.

5. Talk regularly. Over time, assumptions and unmet expectations can creep into marriage, even in the area of finance. Talk about where you are with your budget (yes, you need one!). Share with each other any upcoming needs or wants (like a concert or a retreat) and evaluate how you could work together to make it happen.

Reflect

Which of these suggestions would help you and your spouse as you talk about finances?

What adjustments do you feel like you need to make in your attitude toward money?

Respond

How did God speak to you today?

What is your response to Him?

Day 4
Great Sexpectations

1 Corinthians 7:1-7

While at a girls' get-together several years ago, the topic of sex came up. The conversation went something like this, "Ugh, honestly, I could take it or leave it." And another gal chimed in, "If I could lose this extra weight, I would probably like it again. My husband said it doesn't matter to him, but it matters to me." Still another gal shared, "I just don't understand why they want it so much! Get over it!"

All of these women are in committed Christian marriages. We all love our husbands very much. Some of us have been married in the single digits; others, for much longer. But around the circle that night, we were all unable to understand our husbands' appetites for sex. Significantly, we all struggled to adapt to their appetites and match desire with desire. We all admitted to times when sex felt more like a duty or a chore than a passionate pursuit.

When my kids were young and extremely needy, sex became a mere afterthought in my marriage. My unspoken logic amounted to "Hey, there's only so much of me that can go around. Sorry, hubs, but you're the only one in this bunch who stands over two-feet and can fend for yourself, so get in line—behind the infant in need of a diaper change, the toddler with the unexplained rash, and the kindergartner who's responsible for selling 30 pounds of cookie dough for the T-ball team by tomorrow's practice."

On many days, I counted the hours until the kids' bedtime. So did my husband, but for a different reason. Finally, I would arrive at that magical moment when I would collapse into the bed, thankful to have survived yet another day, only to glance over at my husband and be met with "the look." You know the look I'm talking about. The "I need you" look. And I would usually give him a look back that says, "Touch me and prepare to die."

I'm betting you can relate. Most of us are just too distracted, exhausted, emotionally spent, and completely drained to make sexual intimacy a priority.

Recall

When you were young, what was your view of sex? Did you have any false notions of what sex was like? What fables or old wives' tales were you told?

When you look back over your marriage, how has your sexual relationship with your husband changed for either good or bad?

Read

A chapter on marriage would be incomplete without a discussion of sex. There. I've typed it. *Sex*. Did you look around you in the coffee shop to see if anybody noticed you reading about sex? Do you feel your neck growing red? What is it about that subject that makes us cringe? Perhaps it's because we live in a culture that is obsessed with every possible distorted expression of sexuality. And maybe it's because church culture has reacted against those distorted expressions, making a person seem somehow less holy for having sexual needs.

For just a moment, let's put aside our preconceived notions, fears, and anxieties about the topic and look at God's Word to see what He has to say.

Read 1 Corinthians 7:1-7.
What was your first reaction to these verses?

What do you think Paul was trying to say?

What verses were most significant for you?

What do you glean about God's perspective on sexuality?

To fully understand Paul's instruction here, you'll need a little background on the church at Corinth and this letter to them. Paul was writing for two reasons:

1. to correct some of their faulty theology and behavior; and

2. to answer some questions they had sent in a previous letter.

The other bit of information you need pertains to the city of Corinth itself. Think of it as a New Testament Sodom and Gomorrah or an ancient version of America today. A temple to the goddess Aphrodite towered above Corinth. In the evening, the temple priestesses would come down into the city. These priestesses were actually prostitutes who would meet men for sex, and a portion of their wages supported the temple. Sexual immorality was rampant in the city.

Also popular in Corinth was a teaching called gnosticism. This stream of thought said that everything material is inherently evil and corrupt, including the body. This resulted in one of two reactions:

1. A person could do whatever he wanted with his body because the body didn't count. It is totally evil anyway and only the spirit matters, so he could express himself sexually any way he desired. We call this view hedonism.

2. A person could deny all of the natural things the body was created for, including sexual expression. Even if a person was married, he should restrain from sexual relations because everything in the body is evil. We call this view asceticism.

Paul was trying to tackle two problems at once: the sexual immorality that resulted from temple worship and the gnostics who were either wild or abstinent. He sought to address a wide range of people and establish a healthy understanding of sexuality.

So what was Paul's response? Simply put, sexual relations are good—within the boundaries of marriage. That's what these verses are talking about. Keep in mind that Paul is no lyricist (like Solomon), so his description of sex within marriage is, well, less than poetic. But he does make his point: the marriage bed is a place of giving and receiving, of meeting each other's needs, of actually serving and satisfying each other.

Notice I said *mutual*. The Bible does *not* teach rape or forced sex as an act of submission. These verses are *not* a proof text of sexual exploitation.

Sexual intimacy between husband and wife is an act of love, not power. In fact, Paul compared the unity between man and woman to Christ and the church (check out Eph. 5:31-32).

What does this mean for you and me? Well, that depends on the health of your sexual relationship with your husband. You may have a great sex life and this is just a reminder. For some of you, though, it may mean a major adjustment in your marriage. A good question to ask yourself is, *what's driving your sex life? Is it fear? Anxiety?* (I get it ... being naked can be scary.) *Resentment? Drudgery?*

If so, then at least you need to sit down with your husband and have a very honest talk. You may need to talk with your doctor if physical pain is hindering your sex life. Or you may need to talk with a therapist. Believe me, your marriage is worth the embarrassment you may initially feel.

For all of us, it probably means shedding the idea that being holy means we don't feel sexual desire. After all, God created the sexual organs, including their pleasure centers. He could have created biological tools for reproduction only, but He didn't. He intended for us to enjoy pleasure.

Don't let culture dictate your sexual health. If you are married, then by all means enjoy the gift God gave you and your spouse. Let loose a little. Turn off the TV and put on something sexy. Pursue your husband. He won't think you're bad or naughty or sinful or unholy. He'll *love* it. Trust me on that one.

And if you need help dealing with physical or emotional barriers, then get it. Soon. Your husband is worth it. Your happiness is worth it.

Reflect

What have you learned today that will change how you approach sexual intimacy?

Is your relationship with your husband somehow less than you (or he) would like? Explain.

What actions do you need to take to develop a healthier sex life?

Respond

How did God speak to you today?

What is your response to Him?

Day 5

And in This Corner…

Ephesians 4:29–5:2

When Keith and I were newlyweds, we took a trip with another couple to Disneyland. Keith had just wrapped up his final year of law school and taken the bar exam. He was due to start his first job a couple of weeks later, so we planned the trip as a celebration and the beginning of a new chapter. I had never been to a Disney theme park, so was looking forward to the experience. It was everything I had hoped it would be—that is, until the last hour.

Along with our friends, we gathered on Main Street in front of Magic Kingdom to wait for the evening fireworks display. We had a prime spot at the front of the crowd, and our friends asked if we would hold the spot while they went into a nearby shop to get a T-shirt to commemorate the day. We had some time before the show began, and they offered to get back in time for Keith and me to shop for a souvenir as well. We agreed and off they went.

Now, I should divulge that I am a souvenir junkie. Anytime my family took a trip or went somewhere special, a souvenir was part of the package. It didn't matter if it was a school field trip to the planetarium or a trip to the carnival in the parking lot of the grocery store—a souvenir was in order.

At the beginning of the adventure, my dad would hand my brother and me a predetermined amount of money for the sole purpose of purchasing a souvenir. T-shirt, back-scratcher, stuffed animal, one of those giant oversized pencils—anything was fair game. (One of my favorites was a tiny drinking glass that I found in the gift shop at the Fort Worth Zoo while on a elementary school field trip. I was into miniatures and thought it was so cute and perfect for one of my staged tea parties. I later figured out it was a shot glass, but who said you can't put tea in a shot glass?)

So, fast-forward to Disneyland and my forthcoming souvenir. Unfortunately, Keith missed the memo stating that souvenirs were a nonnegotiable when taking trips or visiting special places. After our friends left (to get *their* souvenirs), he made

some comment about overpriced gift shops, blah, blah, blah, price-gouging consumers, blah, blah, blah, the family budget, blah, blah, blah.

What happened next could best be described as World War III on the curbside at Magic Kingdom. We didn't scream at each other, but we traded plenty of barbs as we whisper-yelled our point of view. It didn't help when our friends returned wearing their new Mickey and Minnie sweatshirts. And holding a funnel cake.

My husband eventually came around and relented, but by then, I was no longer interested. I explained (with clenched teeth and dagger eyes) that I didn't want a souvenir to remind me of this "awful day" and our fight in front of Magic Kingdom.

In hindsight, the fight seems so trivial and stupid, but at the time, it represented how ill-equipped Keith and I were at conflict resolution. We had no idea how to fight fair.

Recall

Write down all you can remember about your last silly argument. What was it about? Did anyone "win"? How did you feel afterward?

Who is the better debater—you or your husband? Why?

Have you ever argued over something really, really stupid? Explain.

Read

Scientists tell us that diamonds are forged about 100 miles or so below the surface of the earth. There, the weight of the overlying rock combined with high temperatures bearing down on carbon atoms lead to the formation of diamond crystals.

Because of the high pressure and high temperature, these carbon atoms will affix to each other in a very strong type of bonding. That's why a diamond is so hard—it is created because of very, very strong covalent bonds that form between carbon atoms.

That process is a beautiful parallel of conflicts and arguments in marriage. When heat and pressure bear down on a couple in an argument, the two people have the opportunity to bond together so tightly that their marriage becomes like a diamond—incredibly beautiful and virtually indestructible.

Unfortunately, many couples have never learned the art of arguing to a positive outcome. In many cases, the heat and pressure caused by conflict actually pushes couples apart. Is it possible for a couple to argue with each other and come through on the other side more in love with each other? Can respect and love be a part of disagreements? Is being right or wrong the only option in an argument?

Read Ephesians 4:29–5:2. This passage is often used in reference to relationships with fellow believers. However, they also apply to the marriage relationship.

When thinking about your marriage, which of these verses most stand out to you?

What would unwholesome talk look like in a marriage?

How does your husband need to build you up?

How do you need to build up your husband?

In what ways might the Holy Spirit be grieved in your marriage?

For these emotions, record how each can be fueled in an argument:
Bitterness

Rage

Anger

Slander

Malice

Why is it easier to forgive someone else than to forgive your spouse?

What would imitating God look like in the midst of an argument?

What does it mean to "walk in love" (Eph. 5:2)?

Based on these verses, what ground rules for arguments could you implement in your marriage?

Paul outlined basic rules for how to get along—and how to fight well. These verses are also a blueprint for healthy relationships. What he talked about is the basic stuff we teach our kids but somehow forget to apply in marriage.

1. Don't use bad words (Eph. 4:29). The Message says, "Let nothing foul or dirty come out of your mouth." The word "unwholesome" (NIV) actually means "of poor quality; bad; unfit for use; worthless."[2] In other words, if you can't say something nice, don't say anything at all.

2. Don't tear down (4:29). The word "edification" (NKJV) means "to promote another's growth."[3] So when the two of you argue, are your words intended to help your spouse grow or to tear him down? Be honest with yourself; you know your motivation.

3. Don't make God sad (4:30). If what you say to your spouse would hurt God's heart, try another approach.

4. Don't stay mad (4:31). Isn't that what Paul meant when he said, "get rid of all bitterness, rage and anger" (NIV)? Don't slander and malice grow when anger goes unchecked? Once the argument is over and you have settled the issue, anger has no place. If you are still peeved, then do a gut-check to figure out why. Something deeper may need attention.

5. Be kind (4:32). Enough said.

6. Let it go. Forgive (4:32). Do you hold grudges against your spouse, making him pay for a mistake he made months ago? Do you hold forgiveness over your husband, manipulating him into doing something you want? Christ's forgiveness granted to you is unconditional.

7. WWJD (5:1)? Don't roll your eyes at this reference. I know it sometimes is overused, but that's really what Paul had in mind in Ephesians 5:1— "be imitators of God" (ESV). The Greek work is *mimetes*. Look familiar? Lop off the last three letters and you get "mime." What would miming God look like

in marriage, in an argument? "Blessed are the peacemakers" (Matt. 5:9, ESV). "Father, forgive them" (Luke 23:34, ESV). "Has no one condemned you? ... Neither do I" (John 8:10-11, ESV). Like Father, like daughter. Mimic Him.

8. Love (5:2). The word Paul used is *agape*, which is the same word used of Christ's love for us. In other words, love like Jesus loved. Freely. Without condition. Openly. Relentlessly. Stubbornly. Without hesitation or reservation.

Aren't these the basics we teach our kids about getting along with others? So why don't we follow those rules when we argue with our spouse? Perhaps because our pride and agendas get in the way. Is the purpose of your argument to put down your spouse? To prove that you're right? To get your own way? Are you in this conflict because you've allowed anger to creep in? Because you still harbor resentment and can't quite forgive?

Arguments are a part of marriage. Two people + two personalities + two histories x years of life together = disagreements. Lots of them. But as the adage reminds us, the key to a great marriage is a short memory. Leave the past where it belongs and move forward, allowing the pressure and heat of your arguments to forge a diamond-solid marriage.

Reflect

How does today's encounter with God's Word change your perspective on arguments in your marriage?

Respond

How did God speak to you today?

What is your response to Him?

week 4

parental guidance needed

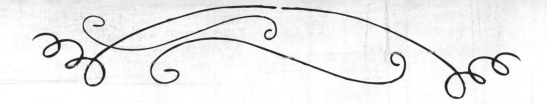

"Most of the people who will walk after me will be children, so make the beat keep time with short steps."

Hans Christian Andersen

(Hannah to Eli) "I prayed for this child, and the LORD has granted me what I asked of him. So now I give him to the LORD. For his whole life he will be given over to the LORD."

1 Samuel 1:27-28, NIV

DVD session 4

Lyndsey Testone, Kati Smith, Anna Jenkins, Shelly Gleason

QUESTION: As a mom, do you struggle with feeling like you're not good enough, not doing enough, not being enough for your children? If so, in what ways?

One way we buy into this mind-set is by believing _____ _____ that good mothers expose their children to every activity under the sun. I'm still apologizing to my adult children.

QUESTION: Can you think of a time when you felt pressure to get on the Mommy Fast Track?

The root of the problem is, as mothers _____ _____ _____ _____ _____ for our children living happily ever after.

At the end of the day, is more really less?

Luke 10:38-42: "one dish is sufficient"

QUESTION: In what ways might your current parenting philosophy change if you embraced the attitude that "one dish is sufficient"?

How can our kids "be still and know God" if we're running them all over town?

Mark 8:1-8

Takeaways for weary mothers:

1. Bring Jesus what you have.
2. Trust Him to make it enough.

If I could, I would tell my younger-mom self:

- to stand over the crib and watch that baby sleep just a few minutes longer

- to go on more weekend getaways with my husband and not worry so much about the kids when I do

- to let my children climb more trees and skin more knees

- to not nag my oldest son so much about getting a haircut, even though his bushy hair helmet could justify its own zip code

Most of all, I'd tell my younger-mom self that all those times that I felt I wasn't a good enough mother, God had my back.

Discuss together

If you were granted a parenting do-over, what would you tell your younger-mom self to do differently?

What challenge are you facing that you could bring to Jesus and trust to His sufficiency?

Downloads of this session are available at *www.lifeway.com*. *Bonus: Check out the segment on Anna's journey with infertility.*

Day 1

Keep Your Eye on the Prize

Deuteronomy 6:4-9

When my oldest child was four years old, Keith and I signed him up for a Pee Wee soccer team in our community. My husband and I both played sports and felt it would be good to expose our son to team sports at an early age. Only one problem—my son refused to play.

He hated practice, begged to quit, and stood on the sidelines, refusing to play. Every. Single. Game. We begged. We pleaded. We bribed. But to no avail. He just wasn't interested. We eventually let up on him and chalked it up to a lesson learned. A lesson, truth be told, that would be relearned over the years.

By the time he graduated high school, he had racked up plenty of experiences with team sports (football and basketball), and we didn't even have to resort to bribery. When I think back on how much time and effort my husband and I spent trying to convince him to play soccer at the age of four, I want to go back and slap us both silly. Today, we all laugh at the pictures of him in his spotless soccer uniform alongside his sweaty teammates with grass stains on their shin guards.

For the record, my boy now has a son of his own and one of his favorite things to do with him is—yep, you guessed it—kick the soccer ball around in the backyard. My grandson is barely walking, but my son has already taught him how to kick a soccer ball and has said he cannot wait until he's old enough to play on a team. Oh boy. Here we go again.

Recall

When you were a child, do you remember pressure from your parents to be successful at something, like school or a sport? How did you feel?

How did that pressure shape the way you parent now?

How have you been pressured lately to push your children toward success in some area?

Read

It is impossible *not* to feel the pressure to create highly successful, highly productive children. Just look at any newsstand or peruse any child-rearing section of a bookstore. Google the phrase "successful parenting" and you'll be confronted with more than 50 million results. Fifty million. And every one of those sites will tell you something different about what makes you successful as a parent. Is it shaping a compassionate kid? A well-rounded adult? And what does it mean to be well-rounded?

It's enough to make you want to sell your suburban plot, move to the mountains, and raise your children to live off the land. But then, how would you know if you've been successful at that? I guess if your kids don't starve ...

The truth is, culture defines the parent role differently than the Word of God does. Early in Israelite history, God set forth His standard, His goal for parents as they rear their children.

> Read Deuteronomy 6:4-9.
> What did God mean when He said, "The Lord our God, the Lord is One"?

What was the command given in verse 5?

Based on verse 6, what were the people of God supposed to do with these decrees or statutes from God?

Verses 7-9 provide the primary command for parents. What is it?

These verses contain some of the most famous verses in Jewish culture. Verse 4-5 are the Shema, the basic Hebrew (Jewish) confession of faith toward God. This prayer is cited both morning and night, as well as during holidays and at deathbeds. The phrase "The Lord our God, the Lord is One" is an affirmation that Jehovah God is the one true God. Remember, the Israelites were living in a land filled with pagan gods. This phrase reinforced the truth that He is the true God and not some pantheistic spirit of the universe. Unfortunately, the Jews often failed to live up to the Shema and began to adopt the practices of the culture around them (remember the golden calf incident?).

If you think about it, this basic affirmation is just as important today as it was in 1400 B.C., the approximate time Deuteronomy was written. Look around you. Our world is full of false gods. False sources of hope. Faulty means of salvation. In fact, the trend is toward faith in any belief system rather than an assertion that God alone is the one true God. Our faith is too exclusive to many. Divisive. Picky. Demanding of a choice. Black-and-white in a world of grays.

But the Scripture is clear: our role as parents is to teach our children that God Almighty is God alone. Nothing else takes His place. There is no substitute. No "all gods are really the same God." No "it doesn't matter what you believe as long as you are sincere." I can sincerely believe that my eyes are yellow, but I would still be wrong. If you're not teaching your children to affirm the biblical God as the only God, then start there.

If you've done that, you're still not off the hook. There is much, much more to successful parenting. But it has nothing to do with scholarships or civic awards. It's about loving that One true God—completely.

Did you notice the repetition in verse 5? "With all." With all your heart. With all your soul. With all your strength. Now, we could spend a lot of time breaking down what the words "heart" and "soul" and "strength" mean, but knowing the nuances doesn't change the overall picture—love God with all you are. As much as you can. In abundance.

Notice that God did not say, "Teach your children how to balance living in the world and loving God simultaneously." He did not command parents to rear cultur-ally acceptable and likable children who would be voted most likely to succeed. He did not tell them to teach their children over and over the importance of getting good grades in school. He commanded parents to teach their children to love God. With full force.

How do we know it was the most important command? Is there any other Scripture that was to be "on your heart" (v. 6, ESV)? The command against adultery isn't top priority. Neither is tithing or telling the truth. It wasn't even a command to remain sexually pure until marriage. Why not?

Because when you teach a child to love God above everything else—above people, above prestige, above boyfriends or girlfriends, above GPAs and SAT scores—then the rest falls into place.

The problem is that sometimes we parents are focused on the wrong thing. We're so busy teaching them correct behavior that we've forgotten that what matters is their character, a character forged from a biblical, godly worldview. We've com-partmentalized God to a discussion between our children and their Sunday School teachers instead of making faith an ongoing dialogue that occurs around the table at dinner, in the van on the way to practice, and on vacation at the beach.

That's what verses 7-9 are all about. God commanded His people to pass on their faith to the next generation. Not by offering a discipleship class but by teaching it in every life situation, day after day.

The truth of the matter is this: you may raise your children to be moral and ethical people, but if you have failed to demonstrate what it looks like to love God with all you are, then you've been focusing on the wrong goal. Nowhere does Scripture highlight success. It calls for faithfulness to God based on love for Him.

And in the end, your children's relationship with God is the one thing they can cling to, no matter what. If you can teach them that, then you're on the right track.

Reflect

How would you describe your pursuit of teaching your children to love God with all they are?

Do you think your children see you loving God with full force? Explain.

What might you need to do differently to place more focus on loving God as a family?

Respond

How did God speak to you today?

What is your response to Him?

Day 2

Bringing the Helicopter in for a Landing
Genesis 27:1-17; 25:22,26,28-34

I am a recovering helicopter mom. There, I've confessed it. I wasn't the type of helicopter mom who double-checked my kids' homework and wrote their admissions papers for them. However, I hovered over other details of their lives.

I remember getting a wake-up call when my daughter went away to college. She attended college out of state, more than 800 miles away. Prior to leaving for college, she had never been away from home for longer than a week for summer camp. And then, just like that, she was gone. It was hard letting my older son go, but my daughter leaned on me more to help her out with the little details in her life. Like when she had a doctor's appointment in her first semester and she was nervous to go alone.

Helicopter mom to the rescue. She called me while filling out the paperwork and I walked her through the forms. Insurance provider: check. Group ID number: check. Emergency contact: Duh. I mean, she was only 18—she needed her mother's help, right? But, here's the worst part: I had already Googled possible medications for her condition and noted a few with some risky side effects. I told her to text or call me if the doctor mentioned prescribing one of the medications on Mama's No-No List. Sure enough, I got a call from my daughter: the doctor wanted to prescribe one of the medications on my list.

After a few minutes of my daughter attempting to relay my concerns to the doctor, I finally asked her to put the doctor on the phone, so I could ask questions about the diagnosis. The doctor politely explained that my daughter would have to grant her consent to talk about the medical visit because my daughter was eighteen and no longer a minor. Excuse me? We're talking about my baby girl here, Missy!

When I hung up the phone, I felt rather silly. After sulking a bit, I realized it was time for me to step back and allow my daughter to grow up. After, of course, I helped her figure out what classes to take in the spring. Only kidding.

Recall

When's the last time you micromanaged or "fixed" a problem for your child? What happened? Were there any consequences as a result?

What did your child learn (or not learn) from that experience?

Read

Spend any time on satellite or cable television and you'll see plenty of examples of helicopter moms. (Helicopter parents are named as such because, like helicopters, they hover around their kids, making decisions for them and "guiding" them even when kids need to take charge of their lives.) We've all been guilty of it one time or another. But sometimes, it can go to extremes, like the parents who contacted their offspring's employers to negotiate salary and relocation package. I'm not making this stuff up, I promise.

It seems like helicopter parenting has reached its peak in recent years. But what if I told you that helicopter parenting has been around for a long, long time?

> Read Genesis 27:1-17. Pay special attention to Rebekah's relationship with her son Jacob.
> What can you recall about the relationship between Esau and Jacob?

What did Isaac request of his son Esau?

Who was listening in the wings? What did she do?

What do you think motivated Rebekah to get involved?

How did Jacob react to his mother's involvement?

Let's look back just a bit. Esau and Jacob are famous for fighting with each other. In fact, Scripture records that "the children inside her [Rebekah] struggled with each other" (Gen. 25:22). They came out of the womb with Jacob grabbing Esau's heel (25:26), the first-ever wrestling match. Scripture also records something very interesting: "Isaac loved Esau because he had a taste for wild game, but Rebekah loved Jacob" (25:28). Now if this brood doesn't win the award for Dysfunctional Family of the Year, I don't know who would.

If you remember, Esau sold his birthright to Jacob for some stew (25:29-34). In the Old Testament, the oldest child received a double portion of a man's inheritance along with the father's role as head of the family. In a moment of stupidity, Esau gave up the double portion in exchange for food. Clearly, he was not a wise or disciplined man.

Fast-forward a few years. The boys are all grown up and their dad is about to die. You'd think they'd show a little maturity at this point. Nope. Isaac summoned Esau to go out into the field to kill some game, cook it, and present it to his father. Then Isaac would bless Esau.

Rebekah enters the picture and fixes things like any helicopter parent would do. Remember, Jacob and Esau are all grown up. Jacob is wearing his big-boy britches and should be able to handle this situation on his own. Perhaps Rebekah told Jacob because he wasn't privy to the conversation, but I doubt it, based on what she does throughout the story.

Rebekah cooked the meal for Jacob (Gen. 27:14). She was willing to let the curse for deception fall on her, removing the consequences from Jacob (27:13). She took Esau's clothes and told Jacob to wear them (27:15). And she put the goat-skins on Jacob's hands and neck. Jacob was called the "Deceiver," but a more accurate title might have been "Deceiver Junior." His mom taught him everything he ever knew.

Rebekah had no business getting involved. As they say in the South, "She didn't have a dog in this fight." But she hovered over Jacob, stepped in, and "fixed it." She even warned Jacob about Esau's anger (who wouldn't be ticked?) and sent him off to live with her brother Laban, covering for him and telling Isaac that she wanted Jacob to go off to her uncle's place so he could marry a nice Jewish girl (27:43-46), unlike his brother Esau (26:34-35). She may have wanted Jacob to marry a fellow Hebrew, but it's clear that her first priority was protecting him.

Now, before you condemn Rebekah, take a long, honest look at your own life. How many of us mothers are guilty of doing the same things? Sure, we're not slapping goatskins on our children (try that and you may land yourself a reality show), but we're great at fixing things. That's what mommies do, right?

In the beginning, it is good and necessary for us to hover and protect. Who wants to watch her child topple down a flight of stairs when he's learning to walk? What mother wouldn't protect her daughter from getting burned by the hot stove? But as our children grow older, we need to back off. They need to learn how to resolve conflict on their own. They need to suffer the consequences of their actions, as painful as that sometimes may be to watch. Our arguing with Johnny's ninth-grade teacher that his *B* really should be an *A* can no longer be a valid option.

The goal of our parenting is to create self-functioning, self-reliant, autonomous adults—not adult children who still cannot think for themselves or act on their own behalf.

Letting go can be painful. It is hard to watch your children grow up. It's hard to watch them suffer consequences for their choices. And if you were honest, you would admit that it's hard to let go and accept that you're not needed anymore—at least in the same way you once were.

But if you don't do the hard work of letting go, you're not really helping them. You may think you're doing the right thing, but in the end, you're really doing more harm than good. We must graduate from kissing their boo-boos to pointing out where to find a box of bandages.

Reflect

How do you feel when you think about backing off and letting go?

What life lessons does your child need to learn that you've thwarted because you intervened?

Respond

How did God speak to you today?

What is your response to Him?

Day 3

Worldly Distractions

Hebrews 12:1-2

While recently flipping through an old photo album, I found a picture of my family standing outside church on Easter. The kids were little and dressed in cute, matching outfits right on down to my daughter's hair bow that blended perfectly. (For the record, what I called "cute," my boys later called "an assault to their manhood.")

The picture immediately triggered a negative memory of a season of life that I'm not proud of. In the weeks leading up to Easter, I'm ashamed to say that I spent more time dwelling on what my children would wear than on the actual meaning of Easter. But that's not all. There were egg hunts to plan and Easter baskets to fill, because heaven knows that's what Easter is all about. Not. I can't remember exactly what our pastor preached on that particular Easter, but I do remember God nudging my heart with a deep conviction over my misplaced priorities.

That wouldn't be the last time I received the Lord's gentle nudge regarding misplaced priorities. The nudge would come again when I got a bit too invested in my children's sports activities. And again when I went overboard buying gifts for my children at Christmas. And yet again when I found myself finishing one of my son's school projects so that it would be on par with the other mothers' projects.

When I did get the divine nudge, God would allow me to see the foolishness of chasing after the world's prizes. I would feel deep regret and pledge to change. And for a time, I would succeed in refocusing my priorities on things that mattered for eternity. Until I would be lured away again to another worldly distraction.

Recall

If you were to be brutally honest, what earthly distractions pull at you the most?

What things of this world tempt you most? Reputation? Appearance? The approval of others? Perfection?

Read

"Don't be worldly." Is that just Christianese to you? What does it mean exactly?

Obviously the word "worldly" refers to the biggies: adultery, pornography, theft, alcohol and drug addiction, idolatry, and homosexuality. Those are the topics of sermons every week in church.

But what if you are happy in your marriage and aren't addicted to drugs? Does that mean you're not worldly?

Read Hebrews 12:1-2. Then look back over Hebrews 11 briefly. Why do you think the writer of Hebrews started talking about running a race just after talking about this roll call of faith?

What do you think verse 1 means with the wording "throw off" (NIV)?

What two things did the writer tell us to "throw off"? How are these two things different from each other?

What do you think it means to "run with perseverance"? How is that different than running a normal race?

What does it mean to fix your eyes on Jesus?

How does this passage offer instruction regarding the things we pursue in this life?

The men in our lives love this passage because it is full of sports analogies (insert manly grunt here and hitch up your jeans just a bit). Specifically, the writer focused on "the race." In ancient times, the foot race was the longest and most significant event in the Greek games, so everyone hearing this word of instruction would instantly make the allegorical leap from their current culture to the timeless truths of God.

In the first verse, you and I are challenged to "throw off" a couple of things. There are things we should separate ourselves from, not be united with, and have no relationship or connection with. Our relationship with some things (and people) should be severed completely. Painful, but necessary.

And what are those things? As if on cue, the writer tells us: "everything that hinders" and "the sin that so easily entangles." Hinders what? Our running the race. Our relationship with Jesus. Our pursuing Him. Our following after Him with all of our heart, soul, mind, and strength (Luke 10:27).

Notice the difference between the two categories of things to be thrown off. One of them we can readily identify: sin. If it's sinful, it will hinder your relationship with God, so it's got to go. It will "easily entangle" you. What things trip you up? Those things are distractions from your walk with God. Those are worldly things.

The other thing the writer said to get rid of is "everything that hinders." Notice the broad nature of this term. The writer was casting a wide net, telling us that anything that hinders us from the race we are running needs to go. In other words, something may not necessarily be a sin, but if it hinders your relationship with God, it should be history. It'll weigh you down.

Keep in mind that in the early Greek races, the men ran, well, nude. In the buff. In all their glory. Full moon. Why? Because their long tunics, even when tucked under their belts, made running a long distance fraught with difficulties—lots of chaffing, dropped tunics, tripping, and falling.

Do you get the picture? Worldly things can be the "big sins." And Scripture teaches us to radically cut those things out of our lives (Mark 9:43-47). But *worldly* can even be the not-so-easily recognized traps that aren't sin in the beginning—too much time in front of a screen; too much time spent with another person; jealousy over another mother's all-too-perfect house; a bigger salary.

To be caught up in the world is to have your focus diverted from Jesus, the Author and Perfecter of your faith. He is the central character in your life. He is the one you live for, not something else you can chase after. He is the one who fulfills your every need. The world and the things this world offers just can't make you whole.

When you try to meet the needs of your life—whether physically or emotionally—outside of Him, you're in trouble. Striving to be the perfect mother is worldly. So is pushing your children (or yourself or your husband) to perfection. God never intended for you to keep up with the Joneses or their kids. Or to compare your husband to someone else's.

He wants you to pursue Him, not things that are passing away, to use another churchy term. Money, status, prestige, awards, GPAs and 401(k)s—none of it matters when we get to heaven. The only thing that lasts is our relationship with Him.

I think that's why God paved heaven with gold. He wanted to show us that the things that we value so much in this life are just asphalt to walk on in the next. It's a constant reminder to pursue Him, to run after Him, to keep our eyes on Him as the true Treasure and to guard against being distracted by a cheap substitute.

It's a lesson we need to learn—and to pass on to our children.

Reflect

Do you think it's harder for Christians today, rather than those in other centuries, to keep their eyes on Jesus? Explain.

Do you think Christians in other cultures struggle to keep their eyes on Jesus as much as believers in North America do? Explain.

Which sins are ensnaring you? What needs to be radically cut out of your life?

What other things might be entangling you and distracting you, even though they may not be "sin"?

What cultural things—like Easter or Christmas or even music or fashion—distract you from running your race well?

Respond

How did God speak to you today?

What is your response to Him?

Day 4
Circle the Bandwagons

2 Timothy 3:1-7

I am a sucker when it comes to bandwagons. This might explain a brief spell during which I made baby food from scratch. I decided to swear off store-bought stuff after hearing a presentation by a nutritionist at a mothers-of-preschoolers small group. In summary, store-bought baby food = BAD. As in, sign your baby up for community college because her poor little brain is atrophying with every bite of processed goodness you spoon into her eager mouth. And you, dear mother, will be to blame.

The nutritionist also taught us to read the labels on canned foods while grocery-shopping, because every mother has time for that when her three kids are tossing double-stuffed Oreos and Fruit Loops into the basket at warp speed. I think the nutritionist's point amounted to "Don't bother grocery-shopping because everything in the supermarket is of the devil. Plant a garden and eat what you grow, young, naïve hippie mothers." By the end of the presentation, I practically knocked the other mothers to the ground as I raced out the door and headed to the store to purchase a mini food chopper and fresh fruits and veggies.

At this point, my poor kids had consumed enough processed and packaged foods to put their future SAT scores into the negative digits. Instantly, I got a mental image of my three children lying on a black sofa in a counselor's office as they shared the domino effect of being raised on store-bought baby food. (After they processed the emotional devastation of having a mother who didn't scrapbook.)

As you may have guessed, the make-your-baby-food-from-scratch phase lasted just long enough for me to figure out that (1) my youngest would be eating finger foods by the time I finished making the first batch, and (2) the end result would taste so bland, he would tongue-thrust every precious bite out of his mouth. When this happened, I wanted to scoop up every discarded bite and refreeze them until I could incorporate them into a Thanksgiving dinner casserole.

Heaven knows, I had spent more time making this batch of baby food than any other dish I had ever prepared in my life. Someone was going to enjoy this baby

food if I had to eat it myself for breakfast, lunch, and dinner. In the end, I mixed it into my dog's canned food and even she snubbed it. At the end of the day, I determined that my mental health was of far greater importance than my children's physical health.

Recall

What fads were big in your childhood? Pet Rocks? Atari? Tamagotchis and Giga Pets? Doing the Macarena? Valley Girl talk?

What parenting cultural bandwagons have you seen come and go?

What was the worst parenting fad you ever bought into?

Read

Every generation seems to generate a new parenting fad, whether it be the Baby on Board signs of the '80s or the Dr. Spock method of parenting introduced in the '60s. Some fads are minor—like using glass bottles and green diapers. Other fads, like the trend of breastfeeding children beyond their fourth and fifth birthday, have caused quite a controversy.

Does Scripture speak to the birth and death of fads? Does it say anything about the bandwagons we find ourselves on? Actually, it does.

Read 2 Timothy 3:1-7 (focus on vv. 6-7).

Describe the "last days." What does that sound like to you?

How do you think people or ideas might "worm their way" (v. 6)
into your household?

Why do you think women "burdened down" could be more tempted to
listen to passing truths or fads?

What do you think Paul meant by "always learning and never able to
come to a knowledge of the truth"?

Reading 2 Timothy 3 is like reading the headlines on any online newsfeed. This
culture provides passing fads that promise everything but deliver nothing. And in
the midst of it all are women like you and me who are just trying to do the best
they can as mom, wife, coworker, and friend.

Like the women described in verse 6, we can get burdened down. We can feel the
weight of our own sin, forgetting that it has already been paid for. We can also feel
the weight of daily life, and it sometimes feels unbearable. Am I a good enough
mom? Am I a good enough wife? Can I juggle a career and a family? How do I
make time for myself? How do I do everything (ha!) so that everyone is satisfied
and I am fulfilled? Sound familiar?

With all that weighing down on us, we can fall prey to any bandwagon that prom-
ises a solution that will cure our woe, whether with a smaller waistline or more
obedient children. You can sense the desperation. And those who are out to make
a buck or make a name for themselves can smell that insecurity like blood in the
water. Just watch the daytime advertisements or infomercials; women are inun-
dated with reminders of their failures. Use this brand of fabric softener so your
clothes will be softer (really, how soft can jeans be?). Buy this workout equipment,

DVD, rubber band, special meals, and you'll drop three dress sizes in three weeks. Purchase this book and follow its instructions to parent with love and reason. Scream-free parenting. Free-range parenting. Grace-based parenting. Is your head spinning yet?

In the midst of such confusion, we women will grasp something, anything that feels like it will ground us, give us direction, and help us be better parents. And we can get sucked in. Hook. Line. Sinker. Like many people, we may believe or pay attention to anything if it's packaged the right way.

What is behind it all? Look at verse 6. We're led along by "a variety of passions." The word for "passions" is the same Greek word for "lust" from 1 John 2:16—things we desire, crave, or long for. We long for those things that will satisfy us, which makes sense if you think about it.

As women we give and give and give. Time with our husband. Time with our children. Forty or more hours a week at work. Volunteering at church. We spend our lives meeting the needs of others. Calling a sick friend. Making sure our aging parents haven't fallen or misplaced their medications. No wonder we crave, desire, and lust after having our own needs met! Most of the time we're so exhausted and depleted that we'll look for ANYTHING to meet our needs, fulfill our desires, give us a break, help us out, or give us an edge in conquering the mountain of tasks before us. Enter the bandwagon.

The problem with bandwagons and fads and tricks is that they don't work. They never do. But because we're so desperate for help, for rescue, for solace, we'll allow ourselves to believe that maybe the next time, we'll find the right one. And so we'll jump off one bandwagon right onto the next one, riding a caravan of wagons that run in circles, leading us nowhere.

In verse 7, Paul warned about the consequences of bandwagon-hopping: "always learning" but never really finding "truth." Translation: you skip from fad to fad and in the end, you come up empty because you never acknowledge the truth. What truth? The truth that parenting isn't about gadgets or fads or the latest parenting book or being the best cake-pop-making mom in the class. There are no shortcuts. There are no five magic principles to perfect children. There is no way to organize yourself into being a better mom.

The truth is that parenting is impossible—unless you fall flat on your face and surrender it all to the Father. Only in His wisdom, His strength, His energy, and His guidance can you attempt what He has called you to be as a mom. Notice that I didn't say you'd be the perfect mom or raise the best kids. Not gonna happen because both you and your children are sinners. You may know Jesus, but you are still a work in progress, and so are your children.

Take a look around. If you find you're on a bandwagon of fad parenting, mommy-hood, marriage, or all of the above, just hop off. Then hop into God's Word and stay there. That's the best place to be.

Reflect

What bandwagons have failed you?

How do you think your life would be different if you spent more time with God and less time reading the latest parenting or self-help book?

Respond

How did God speak to you today?

What is your response to Him?

Day 5

Hold On Loosely

Ecclesiastes 3:1-11

I knew it was going to be bittersweet when I moved my last child into his college dorm, but I wasn't prepared for the moments that would catch me totally off guard in the months that followed. Like one Friday evening when my husband and I drove past a football stadium where one son had played.

We saw the stadium lights shining down on the field and heard the echo of cheering fans as the school band played. Both our sons had played football and our daughter had been a cheerleader, so we had spent our fair share of Friday nights in the stands—Friday night lights, as we like to call it in the South. At the time, it was hard to imagine a day would come when we would pack away our stadium seats and cowbells and retire from the stands. But that day did come.

In the midst of the parenting journey, time often seems to either stand still or go at warp speed. There is no in between. And before you know it, the house is quiet. Their rooms stay clean. Their beds stay made. From then on, they stop by for brief visits, but they don't stay (at least that's the plan).

As mothers, we need to allow ourselves to go there and think about that moment. Doing so helps ensure we have the right perspective when rearing our children. They are not ours to keep, but rather to raise for a season. At some point, the bulk of our work is done and we have to release them to a waiting world. It's part of the plan—God's plan. For many of us who invest our entire being into bringing up our children, that moment can be a hard pill to swallow.

Recall

How well did your parents let go of you as you matured?

When you think about letting your children go, what emotions arise?

Read

Nobody likes to let go. It's not in our DNA as parents. It is painful when our daughters no longer want our opinion on clothes. Or help with their hair. Believe it or not, Scripture talks about the rhythm of life, about times for letting go of the things we hold dear.

Read Ecclesiastes 3:1-11.
Which of the "a time to's" means the most to you as a parent?

What point do you think Solomon was trying to make in verses 1-8?

What happens when we try to fight against the "a time to's"?

According to verse 11, how has God made everything?

What does "in its time" mean for you as a parent?

Did you start singing "Turn! Turn! Turn!" by the Byrds as you read this passage? It's hard not to if you grew up with it. While the popularity of this song peaked in the mid-1960s and is largely forgotten or unknown by today's generation, the Scripture on which it is founded is timeless—for every season (turn, turn, turn).

There is an occasion for everything. Birth and death. Sowing and reaping. Weeping and laughing. Embracing and distancing. Tearing down and building up. Searching and giving up. Tearing and sewing. Loving and hating. Mourning and dancing. War and peace.

Most of these situations could apply to parenting. Of course, there's birth. There's lots of mourning and weeping and laughing and dancing. And sometimes you'd like to kill (but you refrain!). Sometimes it's wise to speak and other times it's better to cool your jets and speak later. And there's time for war and peace—they're called the teenage years.

And there is a time—lots of time—to let go.

I know the Byrds' song is referring to a romantic companion, but it applies to parenting. As parents, we live in the constant paradox of holding onto our children while letting them go. How is that possible? Aren't holding on and letting go two different things? Not when it comes to parenting. It's what you hold onto and what you let go of that is the issue.

As your children grow and become autonomous, critical-thinking adults (we hope), you let go—of control. You loosen the reigns so that they begin to take control of their lives, making their own choices and experiencing their own consequences.

That is the long, arduous task of parenting. It is a continuous journey of letting go. It starts from infancy and continues throughout their lives.

When they're babies, you let go of the bottle so they can hold it themselves. Then you let go of the fork. When they are toddlers, you let go of their hands so they can learn to walk without your help. When they learn to ride a bike, you let go of their handle bars so they can ride without assistance.

You let go of the hairbrush and toothbrush so they can learn to care for themselves in the morning. (Unless we're talking sons, and then hang on or they'll never brush their hair or teeth again). You let go of the closet door and let them pick out what to wear so they can dress themselves. Eventually, you'll let go of the credit card so they can purchase clothes for themselves.

You let go of the pencils, school books, and homework. You let go of the car keys. And the friends. And the girlfriends. And the curfew. And ...

While at the same time we let go, we hang on—to the relationship we've built over the years. If we've done a fair job of parenting, the relationship that remains is one of mutual respect and love.

The truth is, we do not own our children. We are their stewards. They belong to God. They are His. And if we hold on too tightly, refusing to allow them to grow and mature, refusing to allow them to make their own choices and experience the benefits or consequences, we are in fact thwarting God's plan for their lives. We are hindering them from becoming all that God created them to be.

Our relationship with our children is supposed to change over time. They're not supposed to need us the same way in their teens as they did in their preschool years. If they did, it would be a little creepy. They're supposed to grow and mature and think independently, even disagree with us.

That prospect can seem scary until you remember that they're God's, not ours. Ultimately, our children are not in our hands. They are in God's hands—God's sovereign, all-powerful, protective, good, and grace-filled hands. And that's the very best place they could ever be.

Reflect

What are some areas you need to release in relationship to your children?

Do you trust that God is taking care of your children—and will take care of them without your help? Be honest.

Respond

How did God speak to you today?

What is your response to Him?

week 5

being part of a bigger story

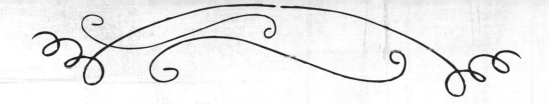

"I want much more than this provincial life!"

Belle in *Beauty and the Beast*

"Imagine yourself as a living house. God comes in to rebuild that house. At first, perhaps, you can understand what He is doing. ... But presently he starts knocking the house about in a way that hurts abominably and does not seem to make any sense. What on earth is He up to?

"The explanation is that He is building quite a different house from the one you thought of—throwing out a new wing here, putting on an extra floor there, running up towers, making courtyards. You thought you were going to be made into a decent little cottage: but He is building a palace. He intends to come and live in it Himself."

C. S. Lewis, *Mere Christianity*

DVD session 5

Today's group: Natalie Bibler, Carrie Betzen, Lyndsey Testone, Anna Jenkins, Tami Overhauser

Reflections in this mirror may be _____ by socially constructed ideas of beauty.

QUESTION: In what ways do you feel pressure to measure up to the culture's narrow standard of beauty?

Proverbs 31:30; Proverbs 20:29: "the gray hair of experience is the splendor of the old" (Prov. 20:29, **NLT**).

Isaiah 45:9-11, ESV:

> Woe to him who strives with him who formed him, a pot
> among earthen pots! Does the clay say to him who forms it,
> "What are you making?" or "Your work has no handles"?
> Woe to him who says to a father, "What are you begetting?"
> or to a woman, "With what are you in labor?"
> Thus says the LORD, the Holy One of Israel, and the one who
> formed him: "Ask me of things to come; will you command
> me concerning my children and the work of my hands?"

QUESTION: When was the last time you stood in front of the mirror and grumbled? What message did that send?

Romans 9:20

Stop, _____ _____, and say out loud to God, "Why did You make me this way?" It puts things in _____ .

Instead of complaining, smile and say: "I will praise You because I am fearfully and wonderfully made. Your works are wonderful; I know it full well."

"Can you imagine opening up your daughter's diary and reading 'Dear Diary, help me to be pretty on the inside'?"
Vicki Courtney in *Ever After*

"Inside every older person is a younger person wondering what happened."
Jennifer Yane in *Ever After*

Discuss together

Who represents the "gray hair of experience" in your life? Why?

Can you recall a time when you got caught up in the frenzy of daily life and lost the purpose behind it all? What was that like for you?

Downloads of this session are available at *www.lifeway.com*.

Day 1

Midlife Identity Crisis

Ephesians 1:3-12

I became a Christian at twenty-one and couldn't wait to change the world in Christ's name. I anxiously awaited my God-given marching orders and nagged Him on a regular basis in my prayer times to reveal His ultimate purpose for my life. Then I got married. I had my first child. I had two more children. I was still waiting.

Eventually, I began to grow discouraged. I began to wonder if my role as wife and mother was supposed to be my primary identity. And I felt guilty for wanting to be more than that. I wanted to influence more people than just my husband and children for the sake of the gospel. If the harvest is plentiful and the workers are few, why didn't God immediately take me up on His offer to serve in the harvest?

Of course, I know now that God knew exactly what He was doing when He tarried in His response. He knew I needed to focus on finding my identity in Him before I raced out to change the world for Him. I had always based my worth on my accomplishments and had mistakenly carried that formula into my new life in Christ. God was far more concerned with who I was than what I did. And this is where so many of us get this identity stuff all mixed up. Desperate to feel worth and value, we sink our identity into titles and accomplishments.

Wife, mom, servant, hard worker, faithful friend, caretaker—we each have a divine assignment, but we must first discover who we are. And it's impossible to know who we are until we know Whose we are.

Recall

Do you ever struggle with how to define yourself? With who you are, really? Wife? Mom? Friend? Sibling? Employee? Church worker?

Record here some of those feelings, past or present.

Think of someone you admire who seems to know who she is. What about her is attractive to you?

Read

It's easy to become confused about who you are. Everywhere you turn, someone is trying to define you by some measure. Are you the room mom who makes cupcakes from scratch and sews her daughter's clothes? Are you the career woman who can't be bothered by such trivial things as cupcakes? Are you the runner who posts her miles and time on Facebook so others can cheer her on? Are you the mom of four who can't imagine having time to run and is jealous of others for their perky Facebook comments about bettering their times?

Do you see how easy it can be to fall into the trap of defining yourself by what you do? It's a slippery slope that leads nowhere.

So where is a healthy place to start? Who are you, stripped of titles and responsibilities and accolades? Who are you, despite past mistakes or current situations?

Read Ephesians 1:3-12.
What stood out to you as you read these verses? In the space provided, list all of the words used to describe you as a redeemed child of God. (I count at least five different words.)

According to verses 4-8, what was God's motivation for saving us?

What do these verses say about your responsibility in God's choosing you and saving you?

According to verse 12, what is the natural result of being chosen by God?

In the original Greek manuscript, Ephesians 1:3-14 actually forms one long sentence. What would cause Paul to get so caught up in writing that he would create such a windy introduction? Think of this opening as the crescendo of a pastor's sermon. Passionate about the content of his letter, Paul was caught up in the magnitude of the message rather than its form. These opening verses of Ephesians contain some of the richest theology and truth in Scripture. Let's break it down.

Verse 4 says that you were chosen before the foundation of the world. The word "chosen" carries the idea of being set apart "from the rest of mankind to be peculiarly his own and to be attended continually by his gracious oversight."[1] You were chosen by Him and for Him. That in itself ought to melt your mind and cause your knees to buckle in humility and worship. That the God of the universe would even choose me in all my mess defies human logic. Praise God for not caring about what human logic would value.

This verse also describes what we believers are—"holy and blameless." These twin words carry similar ideas rooted in sacrifices and offerings. "Holy," as it is used here, means that we are prepared for God as pure and clean. On the other hand, "blameless" carries the idea of being without blemish, fault, or blame.

While that may not seem significant to you and me (being so far removed from the Old Testament and its sacrificial system), being called holy and blameless in the New Testament would have been a big deal. These first-century Christians could now approach God on their own, without a priest and without fear of being destroyed for lack of holiness. Instead of being guilty and flawed and unworthy and unable, these believers could now stand in confidence because God had declared them holy.

If you think about it, you and I get caught in the trap of unworthiness too. Ever feel too sinful to approach God? Ever wonder if you'll mess up one time too many? Ever look at your past and think that He will forgive, but there's no way He could ever really forget and accept you as one of His own? Think again.

I love how The Message paraphrases Ephesians 1:4: "Long before he laid down earth's foundations, he had us in mind, had settled on us as the focus of his love, to be made whole and holy by his love." We are declared whole and holy. Wow. Let that one sink down into the marrow of your soul. It's a game changer.

Did you catch the other words used to describe us? We are adopted as His children (v. 5); we are loved (v. 4); we are redeemed (v. 7). These words do not describe weary, downtrodden, fearful, legalistic people. These are words that invite joy and love and freedom and laughter and hope and peace.

So what was God's motivation? Why did He choose us? Why did He set His sights on us? What made Him pursue us? Verse 5 tell us that it was "in accordance with his pleasure and will" (NIV). Verse 7 gives us another hint: "in accordance with the riches of God's grace." Hearing words like "pleasure" and "will" and "riches of God's grace" ought to shoot adrenaline into the depths of your soul. Why?

Because these words describe God's passionate pursuit of you as His beloved. Notice that there is *nothing* in these verses that describes any work on your part, any merit badge that earns God's love, any action you could take to make God want you. His pursuit is steeped in His grace and in His delight in you.

So what does this mean for your identity, for who you are? It means that you are more than the sum of your achievements. You are more than your latest mistake made or goal reached. Your identity is not defined by your bank account, your weight, the number of friends on Facebook, your children's GPAs or college choices. Your worth is not determined by being a good cook, a perfect house-cleaner (PRAISE GOD), or the cool carpool mom. It's all about what Christ does in and through us. He adopts. He endows our worth. He calls us His own. And nothing can take that away. Who you are is steeped deeply in whose you are.

You are God's beloved. And that, dear friends, is enough.

Reflect

How have you been trying to define yourself outside of God's perspective? What has been the result?

How has today's Scripture changed your perspective of yourself?

Respond

How did God speak to you today?

What is your response to Him?

Day 2

Living with Purpose

Ephesians 1:11-14; Psalm 16:5-11; Revelation 21:3-4

Early on in my Christian journey, I signed up for just about every-thing under the sun in an effort to find purpose. I rushed into the harvest. I tied my worth to my performance and, in my desperation to please God and find His approval, I did what I had always done to find worth: I performed. And I performed. And I performed.

I bet you can guess what came next. Yep, it was your classic case of "growing weary doing good." It's a common problem among believers who want an answer to "Why am I here?"

The heart cry of the human soul is to know the answer to these two questions: "Who am I?" and "Why am I here?" Yesterday, I shared that to know who you are, you must first discover Whose you are. Yet, it's possible to know Whose you are and still get it all wrong when it comes to finding your ultimate purpose.

Once I began to realize that God's ultimate purpose for my life had nothing to do with "doing" and everything to do with "being," my life was forever changed. I got out of the Christian rat race. Climbed off of the holy hamster wheel. Took a breath and realized that God didn't love me any more when I was "doing" or any less when I was "being." I began to respond rather than react to His unfailing love.

There's a difference, you know. Reacting involves actions. Responding involves the heart. Being. Sitting. Knowing. Praising. Oh sure, God has some divine assign-ments lined up for each of us, but they were never meant to be our ultimate purpose. Believe it or not, that's not why we're here.

The most sincere servants are those whose service comes from an overflow of gratitude for who Christ is and what He has done. They respond to His love before they react to His love.

Recall

Can you recall a time when you got caught up in the frenzy of daily life and lost the purpose behind it all? What was that like for you?

Have you ever wondered how to define your purpose in life—beyond being a wife and a mom and an employee? What answer did you find?

Read

Today's culture tells you that your purpose in life is to pursue pleasure or make money. It tells you that your purpose is to be the best—at work, at home, in the bedroom. You can begin to believe that your purpose can be fulfilled by achieving another milestone, by producing the best children, by being the perfect wife for your perfect husband. In reality, those are all "chasing after the wind," as Solomon would say, and also often described as meaningless (Eccl. 1, 2, 4, 6). Your primary purpose for being on this spinning planet we call Earth can never be found in any pursuit or achievement.

To find that purpose, we'll actually be looking at some of the same Scripture you read yesterday.

> Read Ephesians 1:11-14.
> Verses 12 and 14 give you a clue about why God created you and redeemed you. What reason did Paul give?

> Read Isaiah 60:21; 1 Corinthians 10:31; and Romans 11:36 (all ESV).
> What purpose is common among all three of these verses?

Paul was very clear that we exist to glorify God. In that first chapter of Ephesians, he used the same phrase twice (vv. 12,14): "the praise of his glory." What exactly does that mean? It might help to read the phrase in another translation. The NLT says, "Bring praise and glory to God" (v. 12). The God's Word paraphrase says, "God receives praise and glory for this" (v. 14). The Message says it this way: "a praising and glorious life" (v. 14).

Do you get the picture? You were created to bring glory to God. That's what the prophet Isaiah foretold about the people of God. That's what Paul proclaimed in the Book of Romans and challenged the Corinthian church to do. Your life has purpose—to bring attention and fame and acclaim and glory to God.

But there is more.

> Read Psalm 16:5-11.
> How did David describe God in verse 5?
>
>
>
> What did he talk about in verse 6?
>
>
>
> How did David describe his heart in verse 9?
>
>
>
> In the crescendo of this chapter, David described what it was like to be in God's presence. What did he say in verses 9-11?
>
>
>
> Read Revelation 21:3-4.
> How are these two verses similar to what you read in Psalm 16?
> According to these verses, what will eternity be like? Why?

Your purpose is to glorify God. But you have another purpose: to enjoy God. Yes, you read that correctly. Enjoy God. That may rub against everything you ever thought about what the Christian life is supposed to be. Perhaps your Christian experience has been characterized by times of drudgery or check marks for good behavior. Maybe you've been so busy doing things for God that you've lost sight of actually being with God.

David said that there is abundant joy in God's presence (Ps. 16:11). When was the last time you found abundant joy simply being in the presence of God? When was the last time you actually laughed with God? Had fun with God? Felt a sense of joy because you had been with Him?

I think that's why so many people were drawn to Jesus. They actually enjoyed being around Him. It's obvious that the children wanted to be near Him, and children don't like being around mean people. They don't like people with sour expressions and gruff remarks. They like people who like them, who enjoy them, who love them.

Can I dare say this? Loving God is meant to be a joy. It is meant to bring you pleasure.

When you look at Revelation 21:3-4, what mood do you sense? Do you picture the saints of God as miserable? No! God wipes away their tears. He will finally "live with them. They will be His people, and God Himself will be with them" (v. 3). Finally, in eternity, there will be no barriers between God and His people. Finally, they will be together in communion and community. The people of God will finally be face-to-face with the Great Lover, and we will be able to dwell with Him.

If you've been in church for any length of time, you know that you are supposed to glorify God. You've probably hear sermons and Bible studies about it. You've probably read books about bringing glory to Him instead of yourself. But did you know that the primary way to glorify God is to enjoy Him? To delight in Him? To have your life marked by a love for Him that is a response to His love for you? To pursue Him because He has pursued you?

To enjoy being in His presence can take a thousand different forms. It's encountering God in His Word. It is seeing Him at work in the fellowship of believers. His presence can be enjoyed in being fully present with your children. You can enjoy

God by simply being still and quiet. You can enjoy God when you are stunned by a beautiful sunset or the stars that pop out against a dark sky. You can experience His presence in a friend's kind word that came at just the right time or in words from a book that inspire you to great things.

When that happens—when you encounter God in everyday life—you cannot help but fall in love with Him more. And loving God brings glory to Him. It draws others to Him. The world doesn't need more preachers proclaiming the good news. The world doesn't need another church on another street corner. The world needs more people who fall in love with Jesus.

Purpose fulfilled.

Reflect

Have you been trying to glorify God without first experiencing Him? What is the result?

What do you think about the idea that you glorify God by enjoying Him? How is that different from what you've believed or been told?

Respond

How did God speak to you today?

What is your response to Him?

Day 3

Gifted to Serve

1 Corinthians 12:4-11; Ephesians 4:11-12; Romans 12:6-8

In the previous two days, I shared how I initially mistook my purpose in my Christian walk and dove headfirst into the performance game to win God's approval. On my resume of good deeds was a short stint as the meals coordinator at my local church. Have I mentioned that cooking is not my thing? Or organization? Or details? What in the world was I thinking?

I could hardly manage to keep my own family fed, much less organize meals for those in need in my church family. Clearly, this was not my spiritual gift. It wasn't until later in my Christian journey that I learned that God had gifted us each with spiritual gifts to be used for His good and glory. The experience was a stepping stone to discovering my true passions and areas of giftedness. (Hint: Not COOKING! In fact, now I look for excuses to get on the recipient list for the meals ministry: hangnail, sore muscles from a workout, depression over the final episode in season 3 of *Downton Abbey*—I've tried it all.) The point is, God has given each of us spiritual gifts and, sometimes, we find them by process of elimination.

One of my greatest joys in serving as a speaker at events is seeing many spiritual gifts come together for a singular, higher purpose. I marvel at those who have the gift of hospitality and take great care in finding ways to make attendees feel welcome. I love seeing those with a gift for creativity decorate the events to match a predetermined theme. Or those who possess a gift for teaching lead a breakout group. Or those with a gift for organization keep the program on time and running smoothly. (And, for the record, I possess none of those gifts.)

But none of these gifts, including mine as a speaker, is of greater importance than the others. Sometimes, if we're not careful, we can envy the gifts of others and wish they were our own. I recall a speaker friend of mine once saying, "There are plenty of rows to hoe in the harvest. Stick to your own row!" I love it. God reminds me of this wisdom when I find myself looking longingly at my neighbor's row in the harvest and wishing for a different spiritual gift.

Recall

Have you ever felt like you didn't have anything to offer the world?
Describe your thoughts and emotions during that time.

Read

This week has been a progression of sorts. First, you discovered who you really
are—God's beloved. As His beloved, your primary purpose in life is to glorify Him
and enjoy Him forever. Today, we'll discover a way that you can glorify Him and
enjoy Him.

Read 1 Corinthians 12:4-11.
List all that is "different" and all that is the "same" from verses 4-6.

What is a "manifestation of the Spirit" (v. 7, ESV)? Who is given this
manifestation of the Spirit?

List all of the gifts described in verses 8-10. Next to each, write a
definition or example of that gift.

According to verse 11, how is the distribution of these gifts determined?

Read Ephesians 4:11-12 and Romans 12:6-8.

List all of the gifts mentioned in these two passages that are not listed in 1 Corinthians 12:8-10. Again, write a definition or example next to each gift.

Have you ever considered that using your gifts could be a way to enjoy God? Why or why not?

Why do you think there are so many different kinds of gifts? What purpose does that serve?

In 1 Corinthians 12, Paul explained that every believer is given a "manifestation" (v. 7, ESV) of the Spirit. Huh? The Contemporary English Version says that the Spirit has "given each of us a special way of serving others" (v. 7). We often say that God's Spirit has given each of us a spiritual gift. It's something special we can do that glorifies God and strengthens other believers.

You have a gift that the world—and the body of Christ—desperately needs. Your spiritual gift is simply *the intersection of your passions and the needs around you.* As a mom, you are many things: bottle washer, healer of wounded elbows, manager of the home. As a wife, you are your husband's biggest cheerleader and most sacred companion. As a believer, you are a prayer warrior who stands in the gap; the mercy-bearer to those who feel as if God wants nothing to do with them; the teacher who speaks Truth into a world where truth is rarely spoken. I could go on and on.

God didn't intend for you to put your passions and giftedness on hold when you got married and had children or when you went to work. Rather, He wants you to use your giftedness in your sphere of influence. When you use your God-given gifts to honor Him, you'll find a unique sense of joy.

The movie *Chariots of Fire* tells the true story of two British sprinters competing in the 1924 Olympics. One of the characters, Eric Liddell, is a devout Scottish missionary who runs for God. The other, Harold Abrahams, is a Jewish man who runs for fame and to fight anti-Semitism. In one of the most moving scenes in the story, Eric makes this powerful statement: "I believe that God made me for a purpose. But He also made me fast, and when I run, I feel His pleasure."

Joy and pleasure fuel your gifts. Teachers love to research and communicate God's truth with others. People with the gift of mercy ooze a gracious gentleness that just seeps from their spirits. Those gifted with serving find joy and pleasure in working behind the scenes, doing things that nobody but God would ever notice. Preachers cannot help but preach. Encouragers naturally encourage. Leaders feel cramped, hampered, and miserable when they're not leading. Evangelists can't not share the gospel; it's in their bones.

If you're not experiencing joy, you're not serving in your sweet spot. You are not working within your gifts. That's not to say that the teacher of seventh-grade boys will never want to pull his hair out or that offering mercy is always easy. But for the most part, living in your giftedness is a joy. Why? Because you are partnering with the Spirit to serve Him and others. It's just another way to experience His presence, which is to bring you joy (remember what you learned yesterday?).

One last thing: 1 Corinthians 12:11 tells us that the Spirit gives us our gifts as He determines. While you may not understand why God gave you a particular gift, you can rest assured that God didn't just flip a coin to decide to give you that gift. It was according to His purpose. He had a reason. More about that tomorrow.

Reflect

What gifts do you see in yourself? What gifts have other people pointed out in you?

How are you using your gifts?

How do you experience joy in using your gifts?

Respond

How did God speak to you today?

What is your response to Him?

Day 4
I Love Me; I Love Me Not
Ephesians 2:1-10

For years, I have had a magnet on my refrigerator that reminds me, "Happiness is not having what you want, but wanting what you have." If a magnet can preach, this one contains a thousand sermons. I bought the magnet because it contains a truth I need to remember. Every. Single. Day.

Oh, the precious moments I've wasted comparing my house to other houses, my children to other children, my husband to other husbands, myself to other women, and my life to other lives! I can never get those moments back. Of course, I am hardest on myself. I cherry-pick the best qualities I see in others and create a mental prototype of what I wish I could be. There is nothing wrong with wanting to be the best possible version of yourself, but be careful that the goal doesn't consume you and dictate your happiness.

Case in point: for as long as I can remember, I have struggled with body image. Chances are, you can relate. I struggled with an eating disorder off and on in high school, college, and into my early 30s. I became fixated on one magical number on a scale that I saw briefly in my high school years. It became my target goal for nearly two decades. The problem was, it wasn't a realistic number for my height and body structure. Nor did it take into consideration that my body would change after bearing three children (why don't our mothers warn us of this?!).

When I fell short of the mark, discontentment reared its head, dictating my moods and affecting other areas. Regrettably, that is only one battle of many that I fought in comparing my life to others'. Comparison was created in Satan's lab. He knows that those who engage in this battle are focused on earthly matters rather than eternal matters.

Today, I have a healthier perspective in the never-ending battle of making peace with my reflection, though it will always be a struggle for me on some level. God continues to help me see myself through His eyes and celebrate the person He created me to be, freeing me to focus on what truly matters most in this life. (Hint: God!)

Recall

Have you ever suffered from the curse of comparison? How have you compared yourself to others? What have you envied in other people?

Has anything positive ever resulted from comparing yourself to others?

Read

Picture this scene. You and your husband have been invited to his boss's house for a barbecue. Since he's new to the company, you're both anxious to meet others in the group. You arrive and are invited to follow the hostess to the backyard. You walk out the double doors and take in the scene before you. Men and women are mingling, standing around or sitting at tables. Some are playing horseshoes. Others are playing croquet.

In that moment, what is going through your mind? What scenarios are playing out in your head?

If you were honest, you'd admit that at least for a moment or two, you sized up your competition. Of course, that's not what we women call it, but it's what we do. Or comparison. You looked around the yard and measured yourself against every other woman. Is what I'm wearing fashionable? Am I wearing better jewelry? Am I taller? Shorter? Thinner? Prettier? Older? More fit?

And if you were honest, that internal comparison conversation would continue in your head all afternoon. *I'm funnier than she is. I'm smarter than she is. She's better organized than I am. She is more dedicated to her children. I have a better job and a more advanced degree. She's a better housekeeper.*

Busted.

I could change the scenario and the response would be the same. New Sunday School class. Book club. Mission trip. Staff meeting. We women spend countless hours and incalculable energy measuring ourselves in relation to others around us.

So what's the cure for the comparison game? How do we get off the hamster wheel of keeping up with others, running after that elusive "better than" prize that we will never really receive? By taking a deep drink from the well of God's grace. By seeing ourselves from His perspective, not our own.

Read Ephesians 2:1-10.
In the column on the left, list words and phrases that describe you and your life before being saved by God's grace and mercy. In the right column, record everything that describes you now that Christ has saved you.

LIFE BEFORE CHRIST   **LIFE WITH CHRIST**

What word or phrase best describes you before your relationship with Jesus?

What word or phrase best describes you now that you have a relationship with Jesus?

What does verse 6 tell us about our place with Christ?

What does verse 7 tell us about the reason He raised us up to those places?

What word adequately summarizes verses 8-9?

Read verse 10 again, this time in some different translations. What word most adequately describes believers in verse 10?

Creation. Masterpiece. Workmanship. Handiwork.

These words do not describe a dull, one-dimensional being; these words describe symphonies and great works of art. And these are the words used to describe you.

The word "creation" in verse 10 (HCSB) is the Greek word **poiēma**. Does it look familiar to you? That word is the root of our English word "poem."

Taken by itself, Ephesians 2:10 might result in self-inflated ego trips and, well, comparison games. But this verse takes place in the context of Paul describing our relationship with God and to God.

Did you take a look at your life without Christ? U.G.L.Y. Without Christ, you and I are dead objects of wrath, controlled by the flesh and destined for hell. But because of Christ, we are made alive (v. 5). Raised up (v. 6). Riches of His grace (v. 7). Created in Him to do amazing things with us and through us (v. 10). Not in and of ourselves—alone, we're nothing. Because of Him (and *only* because of Him), we are a masterpiece. A piece of poetry that He alone can compose.

This passage is a reminder that we have been created by Almighty God as beings of value and worth and honor. Our response to His creative work in us should be one of thanks and praise, rather than questioning His work, engaging in the comparison game, and wondering why others are so much better, prettier, smarter, wittier, or ...

These verses are very clear: God created you with intent, purpose, and meaning, just as every piece of poetry, every sonata, every sculpture is created. Although you may not understand every aspect of your personality (including your quirks and weaknesses), you can rest assured that God wasn't sleeping on the job when He crafted you. You were not an afterthought in His cosmic plan. He created you with intentionality and in love.

Having the right perspective on yourself can be the key to God using you for mighty tasks ahead. God used David. God used Noah. Moses. Rahab. Jacob. Sarah. Jonah. Peter. Paul. All flawed men and women. All very human in every way, good and bad. And God wants to use you—with every imperfection, gift, neurosis, cowlick, skill, ability, trait, and fear that swim around in that beautiful brain, body, and soul of yours.

You are His handiwork. You are His trophy of grace. You are His image-bearer. He wants to use you.

Yes, you. Just as you are, in Him.

Reflect

How have you seen God use you, in spite of every seemingly overwhelming flaw?

How might your attitude about yourself hinder your usefulness to Him?

Respond

How did God speak to you today?

What is your response to Him?

Day 5
Leaving a Legacy That Matters

Psalm 78:1-8

I wasn't raised in a Christian home, but both sets of grandparents were strong believers. When I was ten years old, my maternal grandparents gave me a children's Bible for Christmas. They lived two hundred miles away, and I didn't get to see them often, but I knew they loved God. When I went to college, I ended up in their hometown of Austin. It was then that I got a view of their faith in action.

They weren't perfect, but they possessed a peace I didn't have. Their faith played a huge part in my decision to follow Christ at twenty-one (at a retreat for college students sponsored by their home church!).

When we hear the phrase "leaving a legacy," we typically think of the positive things we are intentionally passing to future generations. The truth is, everyone leaves a legacy, and it can be good, bad, or just plain irrelevant. I've always liked the phrase "More is caught than taught."

Yes, we need to be intentional about our legacy of faith, keeping in mind that kids will be far more impacted by what they see in our lives than by what we say. Our walk will always trump our talk.

Both of my grandparents have passed away, but I often think of their legacy and the difference it made in my life. One of my greatest treasures is my grandmother's worn and weathered Bible, which sits on a bookshelf in my home office. Beside it is the children's Bible they gave me long ago. When I consider how much I "caught" from my grandparents, it inspires me to be intentional about my legacy.

Recall

What comes to mind when you think of a positive legacy left by your parents, grandparents, or great-grandparents?

What comes to mind when you think of a negative legacy from your parents, grandparents, or great-grandparents?

Read

Whether we like it or not, our lives will leave a footprint for future generations. Our children and their children will either benefit from or bear the consequences of our legacy.

Our spiritual forefathers understood this concept and even wrote about it.

After reading and reflecting on Psalm 78:1-8, answer these questions.

Of whom is Asaph speaking? What "things from of old" was Asaph referencing in verses 2-3 (NIV)?

What "praiseworthy deeds" has God done in your life? How have you seen "his power, and the wonders he has done" (v. 4)?

What statutes was the author referring to in verse 5? (Reread Deuteronomy 6:4-9.)

According to the passage, what was the reason for telling future generations about God's decrees?

When you think about your children—and their kids—what do you want others to say about them (compared to what is said in v. 8)?

This entire Psalm chronicles the history of the Israelite history, and in writing about it, Asaph is modeling for his hearers (and us) the task of communicating how God has worked in the lives of His people. He understood the value of passing faith to the next generation.

When this psalm was penned (around 975 B.C.), the Jewish home didn't contain a copy of Scripture like the typical American home does today. The history of the Jewish people was passed down orally, from parent to child.

The telling of stories and fables in our culture today is largely lost. Although you can find almost any piece of information on the Internet, you cannot transmit the story of your lineage. You can gather data and facts, but only in the oral communication of that story from one generation to the next can you gain a sense of context, meaning, and value.

Think about it: when you were a child, did you ever ask your grandparent to "tell me the story about ..."? You'd probably already heard that story a thousand times, but something within you wanted to hear it again. Why? Because stories root us in time and location and a family. They tell us where we come from and where we are going. They tell us what others have learned—good and bad—and challenge us to live in light of that story.

That's the essence of verses 6-8. Did you notice the reason Asaph gave for telling the next generation the commands of God? It wasn't merely for a badge in Torah School. It wasn't so their children would reflect well on their parents in the synagogue. Telling the story was essential to their relationship with God and their relationship with others.

Verse 7 tells us, "So that they [future generations] might put their confidence in God and not forget God's works, but keep His commands." Isn't that what we want as parents of our children? Is that not at the heart of our taking them to church, reading the Bible with them, praying with them at the dining room table?

We want our children to adopt the faith in God that we have cultivated during their time with us. We want them to trust God, worship Him, and serve Him. We want them to experience the blessings that come from a growing walk with God and avoid the consequences of disobedience.

And as they grow into adolescence and adulthood and begin to think for themselves, our children need to make their faith their own, not just a marred copy of ours. We want to pass on a deeply rooted faith that will sustain them long after we are gone.

As moms, we hold great sway in the faith development of our children. How we approach God, faith, the church, other believers, and matters of theology and the practice of it will ooze onto the belief system of our children. They learn from watching us. (Scary, huh?) As such, we bear great responsibility.

We must be active in the spiritual development of our children. Dropping off the kiddos at Sunday School and Vacation Bible School just won't cut it. Neither will sending our teenagers to the youth minister and hoping that he or she will "fix" them. The church was the second institution God created. The family was the first. That order is highly significant.

Knowing that you will transmit your faith system to your children, whether you like it or not, you need to give serious consideration to what legacy you want to leave. What biblical worldview do you want to leave with them? How do you want them to approach their relationship with God? With fear? Legalism? Insecurity? What do you want to teach them about walking with Christ?

Be purposeful about the legacy you leave behind. In light of eternity, that is all that really matters.

Reflect

What bad legacy from your childhood do you hope to break
for future generations?

What kind of legacy do you seek to leave for future generations?

Respond

How did God speak to you today?

What is your response to Him?

DVD session 6

A Final Challenge: The Dash in Between

Today's group: Jaclyn Benson, Natalie Bibler, Tami Overhauser, Carrie Betzen

The Greek word for "abides" is měnō (men´-o), which means to stay particularly in a state of expectancy. The expectancy this verse is speaking to is to live our lives with an _____ _____ _____ .

John 15:1-11

"joy" = chara (khar-ah´): *cheerfulness*, calm *delight*
"full" = plērŏō (play-rŏ´-o): to *make replete*, to *cram*, to *level* up (a hollow), to *satisfy*. The same word is used in Ephesians 3:19 on knowing the "love of Christ that surpasses knowledge, that you may be filled with all the fullness of God" (ESV).

"Every branch in me that does not bear fruit he takes away, and every branch that does bear fruit he _____ , that it may bear more fruit" (John 15:2).

QUESTION: Is there a time in your life where you felt God's clear presence as you walked through a difficult chapter?

"set" = phrŏněō (fron-eh´to): *exercise* the *mind*; set the affection on. Setting our mind on heavenly things is a _____ we develop. We make sure that Christ is our _____ _____ .

QUESTION: What are some practical steps you feel led to take to make Christ your primary pursuit?

John 10:10

"abundantly" = pěrissŏs (per-is-sos´): (in the sense of *beyond*); *superabundant* (in quantity) or *superior* (in quality); _____ _____ _____ , beyond measure

"Life itself is the most wonderful fairy tale."
Hans Christian Andersen

"You don't always know the last-ever time your child will crawl into your bed when there's a thunderstorm . . . Or the last-ever time your daughter will play with her dolls . . . or your son will play with his Hot Wheels. Mourn these things anyway, after the fact, as they come to mind. And celebrate the new chapter that follows."
Vicki Courtney, *Ever After*

{Jesus said,] "I came that they may have life and have it abundantly."
John 10:10, ESV

Discuss together

How can you choose to "declare joy"?

What role is hope now playing in your nonfairy-tale life?

Vicki concludes this study at, of all places, a cemetery. The location is a good visual reminder that today's life does not last—nor should it be our main focus. The choices we make during the dash in between—that time between the date of our birth and the date of our death—can make a difference forever after.

Downloads of this session are available at *www.lifeway.com.*

Endnotes

Week 1

1. Accessed July 16, 2013, *http://www.blueletterbible.org/lang/lexicon/lexicon.cfm?Strongs=H7592&t=KJV*.

2. Accessed July 31, 2013, *http://www.blueletterbible.org/lang/lexicon/lexicon.cfm?Strongs=H5278&t=KJV*.

3. Accessed July 16, 2013, *http://www.blueletterbible.org/lang/lexicon/lexicon.cfm?Strongs=H5278&t=KJV*.

4. Accessed July 16, 2013, *http://www.jewfaq.org/613.htm*.

5. Accessed July 16, 2013, *http://www.blueletterbible.org/lang/lexicon/lexicon.cfm?Strongs=G2343&t=KJV*.

6. Accessed July 16, 2013, *http://biblecommenter.com/matthew/6-20.htm*.

7. Accessed August 2, 2013, *http://www.blueletterbible.org/lang/lexicon/lexicon.cfm?Strongs=H7592&t=KJV*.

Week 2

1. Accessed July 16, 2013, *http://www.blueletterbible.org/lang/lexicon/lexicon.cfm?Strongs=G4404&t=KJV*.

2. Accessed July 16, 2013, *http://www.blueletterbible.org/lang/lexicon/lexicon.cfm?Strongs=G3029&t=KJV*.

3. Accessed July 16, 2013, *http://www.blueletterbible.org/lang/lexicon/lexicon.cfm?Strongs=G4049&t=KJV*

4. Jon Katz, "Is Technology Killing Leisure Time?" July 11, 2000, accessed July 16, 2013, *http://tech.slashdot.org/story/00/07/05/1930224/is-technology-killing-leisure-time*.

5. "Insufficient Sleep Is a Public Health Epidemic," Centers for Disease Control, accessed July 16, 2013, *http://www.cdc.gov/features/dssleep/*.

Week 3

1. Accessed July 17, 2013, *http://biblelexicon.org/genesis/2-18.htm*.

2. Accessed July 19, 2013, *http://www.blueletterbible.org/lang/lexicon/lexicon.cfm?Strongs=G4550&t=NIV*.

3. Accessed July 19, 2013, *http://www.blueletterbible.org/lang/lexicon/lexicon.cfm?Strongs=G3619&t=KJV*

Week 5

1. Accessed July 22, 2013, *http://www.blueletterbible.org/lang/lexicon/lexicon.cfm?strongs=G1586*.

Leader Guide

by Brenda Harris

Your commitment to facilitate *Ever After Bible Study* will impact your life as well as the lives of women in your group. God wants to challenge, strengthen, and solidify your walk with Christ as you pray, prepare, and guide this study. These suggestions are for six 75- to 90-minutes sessions.

- ☐ Reserve your meeting space (in a home or at the church) and secure a DVD player and television. If possible, position the furniture so everyone can see both the DVD and one another.
- ☐ Arrange for childcare if needed.
- ☐ Promote your study through the church's in-house publications, especially for Sunday School and small groups. Make sure information is on the church's website as well. Design a poster for women's restrooms throughout the church. Create and mail a postcard invitation to all women in the church or to specific target audiences you want to reach in the community. Include details about location, times, and childcare, plus who to call for further information.
- ☐ Gather basic supplies for each session: name tags, markers, pencils, notecards, and extra Bible translations.
- ☐ Enlist a volunteer to provide healthy snacks if desired.
- ☐ Plan to use name tags for the first two meetings; don't assume everyone knows each other.
- ☐ Start each session promptly and honor everyone's time.
- ☐ Pray for yourself and the women who will be in your small group.

Session 1:
Fairy-Tale Letdown

In Advance

Gather various children's books with a "happily ever after" motif (*Cinderella, Snow White, Beauty and the Beast, Princess Fiona, Sleeping Beauty, The Princess and the Pea*, and so forth). Display the books so participants can browse in advance of the session.

Prepare a list of attendees who have already signed up. Allow extra space for others who join the group. Duplicate this list for each participant.

Preview DVD session 1 and identify your own "happily ever after." Each week read Scripture from the video in two or three Bible translations.

Get Started

Welcome participants. Distribute name tags, asking women to write their name and favorite fairy tale on the tag. Briefly introduce yourself. Depending on the size of the group, ask women to explain why they chose their fairy tale.

Read aloud a portion of one of the storybooks. Remind women that our culture promotes "happily ever after" from a very young age. Ask, *What books, movies, magazines, and television programs today present the idea of happily ever after?* (Think romance novels, chick flicks, *The Bachelorette*, and so forth.) *Why are women vulnerable to this scenario?*

Briefly introduce the study, including Vicki Courtney, the format of the book, and each week's group time. Encourage women to find a time and place to study and to commit to the investment of time and reflection needed.

View

Explain the scenario for each week's DVD content: Vicki Courtney is meeting around her kitchen table with women of various ages from the class she and her husband teach. Her DVD group varies slightly each week.

Direct women to the first week's viewer guide (p. 10) and play the DVD. (Decide whether to pause the DVD after Vicki asks women in her group a question to let your group respond, or to hold comments until later.)

Talk About

Ask some of these questions to guide discussion of the DVD content:

- What is the disconnect between real life and the life depicted in fairy tales?
- When was your fairy-tale letdown?
- Explain the difference between "happily ever after" and "happily forever after."
- Ask a woman to read aloud 1 John 2:15-17 from The Message.
- Review the three predominant inclinations of our nature: desire of the flesh, desire of the eyes, and pride in possessions. Ask women to consider privately the area in which they struggle most.

Support and Pray

Distribute the list of names and contact information; update as needed.

Emphasize the importance of confidentiality within the group so that time spent together is a safe place to share and be encouraged. Ask women to commit to pray for each other by name over the next six weeks. Allow participants to share prayer requests. Voice a prayer, asking the Lord to grant insight into His Word and to speak through the pages of the Bible study. Pray for the women and for their requests.

Encourage women to complete week 1 studies before the next group meeting.

Follow up the session by emailing all participants, thanking them for their participation. Pray for yourself and for each woman in the group as you complete the five studies for this week.

Session 2:
Quitting the Family Busyness

In Advance
Preview DVD session 2. Research responsibilities of the Duke of Cambridge, Prince William, and his young son, Prince George of Cambridge. Print an article Vicki refers to—"The Pride of Busyness" (*http://www. relevantmagazine.com/life/whole-life/ features/26793-the-pride-of-busyness*). Highlight portions that speak to you.

Get Started
Welcome women back and introduce newcomers, updating the contact list. Distribute name tags with these instructions: Write your name and the approximate number of miles you've put on your car this week.

Invite participants to share the challenges and rewards of their first week of study. Share your comments about finding a time and location that works and any tips you have discovered that made the study time more productive.

Ask women to share facts they know about Prince William, the Duke of Cambridge. Insert facts you learned when you researched the responsibilities of Prince William and his son, Prince George. Comment that even our lofty ideas about what a prince should do and be are different than the realities of what an actual prince does.

Review
Call for volunteers to share responses to several of these review questions:

- [ ] How do you typically respond when life doesn't measure up to your expectations?
- [ ] How does it make you feel to know that Christ is the only One who will never disappoint, betray, or belittle you?
- [ ] What are your priorities? Are they out of balance? How/why?
- [ ] What is your treasure? What has captured your heart?
- [ ] Have you ever been so busy doing things for God that you didn't spend time with Him?

Remind women of their commitment to confidentiality. Encourage honest sharing but gently ask any person dominating the conversation to summarize her point so others can share.

View

Ask women to find the number of miles we've traveled this week. Ask, *How did your life become so busy? Who is to blame for your busyness?*

Point out the viewer guide for week 2 (p. 42) and watch the session 2 DVD.

Talk About
Guide a discussion of the DVD by asking some of these questions:
☐ When was the last time you were astonished by God?
☐ Why it is so hard to be still before God? What works for you?
☐ Do you suffer from TMC (too many choices)? What's your solution?
☐ Where is your "quiet place"? How does it compare to the never-ending distractions of the world?

Share highlights from "The Pride of Busyness" article and invite reactions. Ask women if they agree with this final sentence: "If the very God who designed us thought that balancing work with rest was worthwhile, perhaps we should give it a try." Ask, *How can we stop the cycle of busyness?*

Support and Pray
Distribute blank notecards and invite women to write a prayer to God, asking for His help in overcoming busyness. Emphasize that these cards will not be shared with anyone. Ask for updates on last week's prayer concerns and invite women to share other requests. Close in prayer for the concerns voiced.

Encourage women as they eliminate busyness and make more time for God this week. Follow up by emailing or calling each participant this week. Build a sincere relationship with each woman and pray for her by name.

Session 3: Marriage Matters

In Advance
Preview the session 3 video and Scriptures. Plan how to adjust the session in consideration of any single, divorced, or widowed participants.

Bring your wedding photos or photos of your parents or other family members. Check the library for a copy of Tim Keller's book *The Meaning of Marriage* and bring it with you to the group time.

Get Started
Welcome women and ask them to share with another participant how this week's study on busyness encouraged, frustrated, or challenged them.

Review
Ask, *How do you know when it's time to get away with the Lord? Have you ever felt guilty for taking time to be alone? Explain.*

Direct women to page 50 where Vicki described being spiritually empty. Call attention to her statement: *Healing cannot really begin until you can* openly admit you have a problem. Ask women whether they identified with Vicki. Encourage them to share some of their stories of exhaustion, overcommitment, and busyness.

Ask for responses to these questions from last week's study: *What do you think the Father would say to you if you were still enough to hear it? What did God teach you on day 5?*

View

Share your wedding photos and any humorous story about your wedding preparations or wedding day. (Option: share humorous scenes from classic wedding movies such as *My Big Fat Greek Wedding* or *Father of the Bride*.)

Point out the viewer guide on page 74. Watch DVD session 3.

Talk About

Encourage women to share but avoid turning today's time into a marriage counseling session. Guide discussion by asking, *When did you discover your prince wasn't always charming? Why does our society place such emphasis on planning a wedding instead of preparing for marriage?*

Display the book by Tim Keller. Remind participants of the value of investing time and energy in their marriages, no matter how long they've been married. Offer to lend the book to anyone who would like to read it. Discuss the

questions from DVD session 3 viewer guide if time allows.

Support and Pray

Add additional requests to your ongoing prayer list. Invite women to form groups of three to pray for requests that were shared and other needs that surfaced during the study time. Remind groups to pray for one another and for the marriages and spouses of those in the group.

Encourage the women to be diligent in their study this week. Follow up by sending a note of encouragement to each woman.

Session 4:
Parental Guidance Needed

In Advance

Preview the session 4 video and Scriptures. As you prepare for this week's session, keep in mind the needs of women who are single, widowed, divorced, or experiencing difficulties with their children.

Get Started

Welcome women back to the small group. Encourage the women to mingle and discuss their studies.

Review

While you want to encourage women to share openly, avoid berating husbands or giving too many personal details. Guide your review of week 3 by asking:

☐ What factors influenced your view of marriage when you were growing up? How is your picture of marriage different now?

☐ How do you feel when you haven't had alone time with your husband?

☐ What suggestions from day 3 would help you and your spouse in financial matters?

☐ While much of day 4 is personal, what did you learn that you could share?

☐ Why is it easier to forgive someone other than your spouse?

☐ What would imitating God look like in the midst of an argument?

View

To make the transition to today's video about parenting, ask, *What grand ideas did you have about becoming a mom? How have those ideas changed since your first child entered the world?*

Ask about children in your group, covering participants' number of kids, ages, and so forth. Acknowledge and encourage women who are expecting, awaiting a finalized adoption, or who do not have children.

Direct participants to the viewer guide (p. 106) and watch DVD session 4.

Talk About

While today's discussion could be intense, encourage honest sharing. Ask the mothers of older youth or adults, *If you could talk to your younger-mom self, what would you say?* Involve everyone in answering some or all of these questions:

☐ In what areas of mothering do you feel inadequate?

☐ How have you allowed culture to influence your parenting?

☐ In what ways do you feel responsible for the "happily ever after" status of your children?

☐ How would your current parenting philosophy change if you embraced the "one dish is sufficient" attitude?

☐ How does it make you feel to know that God has your back as you parent your children?

Support and Pray

Call attention to the list of names and contact information that you distributed at the first session. If some women who started the study have been absent for one or more sessions, ask for volunteers to contact them and invite them to rejoin the group.

Reemphasize the importance of confidentiality. Encourage women to share prayer requests related to their marriage, children, and family. Ask the Lord to speak through His Word this week as women do their Bible study.

Follow up with a group email to encourage women this week. Pray for yourself and each woman in the group.

Session 5:
Being Part of a Bigger Picture

In Advance

Preview DVD session 5 and Scriptures. If possible, bring a toy helicopter. Gather and display several beauty magazines or bring some beauty products.

Get Started

Greet each woman by name today as she arrives. Spend some time interacting with each one as time allows. Begin today's group time with prayer.

Explain that this week's studies have provided a challenging examination of our parenting skills and styles. Display the helicopter you brought and ask, *Do you consider yourself a helicopter mom? Why or why not? Is helicopter parenting always wrong?* Emphasize the difference in loving and caring for your children and hovering over their every move.

Challenge women to share which life stage is the hardest. After a few minutes, point out that the toughest stage is typically the stage we are in or have just completed!

Review

Call for volunteers to respond to three or four review questions from week 4:

☐ When have you felt pressured to push your children toward success?

☐ On page 111 Vicki says: "If you have failed to demonstrate what it looks like to love God with all that you are, then you've been focusing on the wrong goal." Do you agree or disagree? Why?

☐ Have you ever micromanaged or attempted to fix a problem for your child? How did that go?

☐ How do you feel about backing off and letting go of your children?

☐ What things of the world tempt you most? How does your answer affect your children?

☐ What's the worst parenting strategy you've ever bought into?

☐ How do you think your life would be different if you spent more time with God and less time reading the latest parenting book?

☐ Do you trust God to take care of your children ... without your help? Be honest.

Acknowledge how difficult it is for moms to completely trust God with their children. If appropriate, address the challenges of single parenting or potential conflicts when Mom and Dad don't agree on how to parent. Commit to pray for one another in our roles as wives and mothers.

View

Transition into the DVD content by passing around the magazines or beauty products you brought. Ask women to confess which of the beauty products or secrets they buy into or are sold on. Acknowledge that we all want to look our best, but we sometimes have a tendency to obsess about our looks or about aging.

Point out the viewer guide for week 5 (p. 134) and watch the DVD together.

Talk About

Guide discussion of the DVD content with these questions:

- In what ways do you feel pressure to measure up to culture's narrow standard of beauty?
- Describe your understanding of "the gray hair of experience is the splendor of the old" (Prov. 20:29).
- When you look in the mirror, what causes you to grumble?
- What are your thoughts about Vicki's admonition to "stop, catch yourself, and say out loud to God, 'Why did You make me this way?'"

Support and Pray

Review prayer concerns and add new ones as needed. Group women in pairs or groups of three to pray today.

Remind women that next week will be the last group study. Encourage them to finish their studies this week and to take time to review the past weeks' studies as well.

Follow up this week by emailing each participant. Share an affirmation with each woman about how you have seen God at work in her life during the study. Pray for each woman and for yourself as you prepare for the closing session.

Session 6:
A Final Challenge:
The Dash in Between

In Advance

Preview session 6 DVD and Scriptures. Bring back the storybook you read at the first session. Consider providing refreshments for this closing session.

Get Started

Welcome women to the group study. Enjoy refreshments and a time of fellowship before you begin the study. Hold up the storybook you read at the first session and ask, *Did the princess (or the heroine) of this book discover her "happily ever after"? Why do you think so? What might have happened that changed her "happily ever after" to a not-so-happy time?*

Review

Ask several of these questions to review of week 5:

- Do you agree or disagree with Vicki's statement (p. 136) that it's impossible to know "who we are" until we know "whose we are"?
- Think of someone you know and admire who seems to know who she is. What is attractive about her?
- When have you been so caught up in the frenzy of daily life that you lost the purpose behind it all?
- What do you think about the idea that you glorify God by enjoying Him? How is that different from what you might have been taught?
- What are your spiritual gifts? How are you using them to honor God?
- Who has left a legacy for you (good or bad). Explain. What legacy are you leaving for others?

Comment that this week's studies required a lot of soul-searching. Invite volunteers to share discoveries they made or commitments they solidified during this final week of study.

View
Introduce the final DVD segment of challenge and direct the women to page 162 for the viewer guide. Watch the DVD for session 6: "A Final Challenge: The Dash in Between."

Talk About
Guide a discussion of the video content by asking some of these questions:

- What does it mean to "abide" in Christ? Why do you think John

would instruct this 10 times? How can you learn to abide in Christ?
- What does it mean to "live with an eye toward heaven"?
- What's the difference between happiness and joy?
- Are you desperate for God? Explain.
- What do you learn from remembering?

Support and Pray
Challenge participants to privately consider these final questions and to record their responses.

Comment: Vicki mentions that life happens in chapters, some better than others. Consider the time you are in right now. *What parts are hard? What parts are refreshing? What is God teaching you now, and what has He taught you from previous chapters? How will this Bible study impact your legacy or "the dash in between" for you?*

Close with a time of prayer for each woman. Thank God for the study, for the lessons learned, for the difficult realities discovered, and for His faithfulness as we all journey with Him.

Be available after the session to talk further with any participants.

BORN AGAIN

The Bible records a conversation between Jesus and Nicodemus, who approached Jesus at night, curious about the kingdom of God. Jesus told him: "Unless someone is born again, he cannot see the kingdom of God" (John 3:3). Nicodemus responded, "But how can anyone be born when he is old?" (John 3:4).

New birth begins with the Holy Spirit convicting a person that he or she is a sinner. Because of sin, we are spiritually dead. For this reason, spiritual birth, as Jesus described it, is necessary. God loves us and gives us spiritual birth when we ask Him for it.

The Bible tells us all people are sinners (Romans 3:23). Jesus died on a cross and was raised from the dead to save sinners. To be *born again* means that a person admits to God that he or she is a sinner, repents of sin, believes in or trusts Christ, and confesses faith in Christ as Savior and Lord.

Jesus told Nicodemus that everyone who believes or places faith in Christ would not perish (John 3:16). Jesus is the only One who can save us (John 14:6).

To believe in Jesus is to be born again. Confess your sins and ask Him right now to save you (Acts 2:21). After receiving Jesus into your life, share your decision with another person and become involved in a Bible-believing church. Request baptism by immersion as a public expression of your faith (Romans 6:4; Colossians 2:6).

other studies by Vicki

5 CONVERSATIONS YOU MUST HAVE WITH YOUR SON
6 sessions

Millions of boys grow older, but very few become great, godly men. And with so many influences from culture, friends, and celebrities, prepare to talk to your son about the tough topics. Because even though knowing what to say—or how to say it—can be hard, there's no one better to teach him about life, love, and faith than you.

Member Book 005342724 $11.95
Leader Kit 005342723 $149.95

5 CONVERSATIONS YOU MUST HAVE WITH YOUR DAUGHTER
6 sessions

Your daughter is growing up. The world has a lot to say to her, and she's starting to listen. Even if she doesn't quite know it, she needs you more than ever. It's time for you to press in, to tell her some things she might not know (or might have forgotten) about who she is in God's eyes. These five conversations provide the basis for a whole new way of relating to your daughter.

Member Book 005191375 $11.95
Leader Kit 005125844 $149.95

YOUR GIRL: BIBLE STUDY FOR MOTHERS OF TEENS
7 sessions

Raise a godly daughter in an anything-but-godly world by addressing six of the fiercest battles of the teen years: conformity, self-esteem, sexual purity, boys, modesty, and mean girls. Be challenged and empowered to impart a passion for God in your daughter as she grows to become a godly woman.

Member Book 001303671 $11.95
DVD Pack 001303672 $62.95

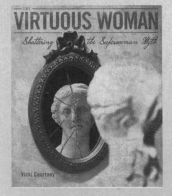

THE VIRTUOUS WOMAN: SHATTERING THE SUPERWOMAN MYTH
6 sessions

For most women, the Proverbs 31 passage offers "more guilt than eating a one-pound bag of M&Ms." Is this the ideal woman? Or is the Proverbs 31 woman an outdated fixture of the past? Unravel the mystery with this study.

Member Book 001114550 $9.95

lifeway.com/vickicourtney
800.458.2772
LifeWay Christian Stores

Pricing and availability subject to change without notice.